LESSONS FROM LaRoux

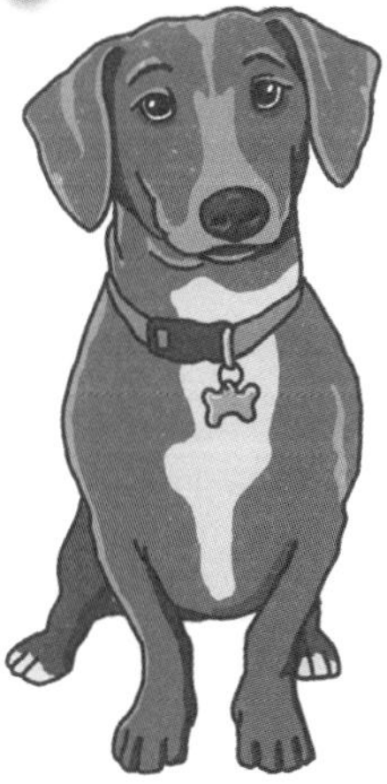

HOW NEEDS SHAPE BEHAVIOR IN DEVELOPING BRAINS

Published by

Duplication and Copyright

P.O. Box 22185 • Chattanooga, TN 37422-2185
423-899-5714 • 866-318-6294 • fax: 423-899-4547
www.ncyi.org

ISBN: 9781953945815
E-book: 9781953945822
Library of Congress Control Number: 2023903699

Written by: Dan St. Romain
Published by National Center for Youth Issues

Printed in the U.S.A. • Chattanooga, TN, U.S.A.
May 2023

TABLE OF CONTENTS

INTRODUCTION

We knew we were in the market for a new furry family member, but we were not expecting it to happen so fast. My wife loves dachshunds, and I wanted a Weimaraner. So, we took it as a sign from heaven when a dog popped up on a rescue site in Louisiana that looked like a combination of these two breeds.

I called to inquire about the pup and was directed to complete an online application. My wife did so, but we genuinely thought the dog would be adopted by some caring family who lived much closer to the shelter than our home in Texas.

Though a dozen others wanted to give the dog a new home, we were the first ones on the list. We had passed the background check, so if we wanted her, the puppy was ours. Fast-forward twenty-four hours, including a twelve-hour round-trip car ride, and LaRoux (Lah-roo) arrived at our home.

My wife and I were excited to spend quality time with our new dog after we had both recently retired from the school system. In doing so, we realized LaRoux needed some behavior modification, so we enrolled her in a puppy class. Our main goal was to get her into good habits while she was still young and open to instruction.

The class instructors had good strategies for shaping the pups' behaviors, but what stood out to me more was their ability to help us, the dog owners, look at behaviors differently. That's when it hit me: This class isn't for the dogs; it's for the humans.

I noticed a distinct pattern during the classes between how the instructors and the owners viewed the dogs' behaviors. I, for one, was guilty of explaining misbehavior through the lens of judgment:

> "LaRoux, you know what you are supposed to do."
> "You're being a little toot! Stop that."
> "You refuse to listen—and you think this is funny. Don't you?"

However, the instructors always reframed comments in a way that took judgment out, providing rational explanations for the behaviors:

> "She's probably confused. We've been throwing a lot of directions at her."
> "LaRoux just wants to play with her friends."
> "Take your dogs for a short walk. They need to get out some energy."

I understood why the instructors took this view; after all, we were working with puppies. However, as I moved through the intermediate and advanced classes, I noticed their perspective didn't change as the dogs got older. They always looked at behaviors through a lens of understanding rather than judgment.

These ladies aren't supernatural dog whisperers, I thought. They are simply good behavior detectives with kind hearts. When problems arose, rather than getting frustrated and chastising the animals, they assumed positive intent and, thus, looked for logical reasons which could explain the dogs' behaviors.

They looked beyond raw behaviors and tried to identify the needs driving them. Once the needs were determined, they focused on getting them met in natural ways that built positive habits and kept misbehavior at bay. I couldn't help but wonder what it would be like if we took this same approach when working with children.

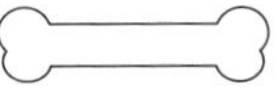

Understanding human behavior is tough, which makes changing it even more difficult. Trust me; I've worked with teachers and parents to improve kids' behaviors for several decades.

Understanding human behavior is tough, which makes changing it even more difficult.

Though I have provided support at all levels, for the past several years, the number of inquiries I've received from early childhood centers, childcare providers, and the younger grades of elementary schools has increased dramatically. The requests usually sound something like this:

"Do you provide staff development on behavior management? We are an elementary campus that services kids through fifth grade, and our teachers are begging for support. Though all the teachers could benefit from some training, our real problems are with the younger students. The lower the grade, the more behavior concerns we see. Our staff is spending all their time putting out fires. I'm not sure what it is, but we've never had so many problems like this."

These calls predictably started rolling in the year after the pandemic. After kids had stayed home for an extended period, providers and teachers faced the reality of what I call "Covid behavioral regression." In other words, kids were not acting their ages.

Adults expected to see some *academic* deficits when the pandemic settled out and kids returned to their regular settings, but the *behavioral* lags caught everyone off guard. Children were demonstrating behaviors typical at much earlier stages of development. One teacher told me, "I have a room full of two-and-a-half-year-old children. But the poor things! They're trapped in four-year-old pre-kindergarten bodies!"

It makes sense that we would see more significant concerns and gaps in younger children simply based on development. The difference between a 38- and 39-year-old adult is not that noticeable. However, the differences are vast when comparing a 12- and 24-month-old child. This is why we've seen more significant lags in younger children. Their lack of experiences and exposure during the pandemic adversely impacted their social and emotional development, which we see through their behaviors.

In these post-pandemic years, kids need support as they work to catch up and acquire the behavioral skills required for healthy development. This book aims to meet this need.

In these post-pandemic years, kids need support as they work to catch up and acquire the behavioral skills required for healthy development.

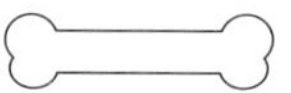

I hear it all the time: "You work with young children? That must be so much easier than with the older ones!" My response is always the same, "Clearly, you have never seen the old Arnold Schwarzenegger movie *Kindergarten Cop.*" *Easy* is not the first word that comes to mind.

Whether or not the work is harder or easier is a matter of opinion. What is important to note is that working with young children is different. *Different* is an important distinction because when trying to support the needs of young children, we can't just modify strategies appropriate for older ones; we must view tasks differently. As adults who successfully work with this population can tell you, development has to be the first lens through which we look when approaching situations.

As LaRoux was working her way through the various puppy classes, the instructors would make a point, and I would find myself thinking the same thing: *That's not about dog behaviors; that's not about kids' behaviors; it's just about what young developing brains need for healthy development.* And that, I discovered, was the key to their successful outcomes. The instructors focused on developmental needs rather than outward behaviors. Puppy training has helped me see how adults often get into the trap of focusing on children's external behaviors rather than the developmental needs which drive them. In doing so, we look at the behaviors with an adult lens of judgment rather than one of understanding and empathy.

This book is designed to look beyond outward behaviors and, instead, at what young developing brains need to survive and thrive.

As you read through each chapter, take a moment to "paws" and reflect on how our actions as adults can often work against our efforts to shape healthy development.

LESSON LEARNED

The brain will get its needs met one way or another.

Behavior in young development serves as communication. Children behave in ways that help them get their needs met. If we can discover the root causes of the needs that drive behaviors, we can be proactive in helping children get them met in healthy ways, decreasing the likelihood of their trying to get them met, often unconsciously, through misbehavior.

I have two requests as you continue reading *Lessons from LaRoux*. First, put on your investigator hat and search for the underlying needs of the behaviors you encounter. And second, adopt the philosophy of assuming positive intent. I believe kids do the best they are able with the skills at their disposal. This approach has never steered me wrong. Hopefully, in doing these things, by the end of this book, you, too, like LaRoux's trainers, will become a great behavior detective.

CHAPTER ONE

EMOTIONAL GROUNDING

When LaRoux arrived at our home, we were happy to see how good-natured she was. Like most puppies, she got along well with our other animals and was very affectionate and social. She was especially friendly to new people and other dogs she encountered. Sometimes she'd get so excited that her bladder failed. This often happened while she ran around our living room, jumping on and off the couch. She couldn't contain herself…literally. This was a behavior we needed to change.

Having had dogs before, we knew what to do. "Bad dog!" we would say, using a stern voice. Outside we would take her, directing her to "do her business" there. Of course, at that point, she really had no business to do. With a confused look and an already empty bladder, she would sit in the grass and wait. Eventually, we would take her back into the house until we faced the same troubling behavior the next time.

LaRoux also tended to put her teeth on people when they played with her. Mind you—I didn't say *bite*. She never clamped down. She did, however, use her mouth like paws. She'd grab people's arms or hands and just stare at them. Though I understood that she wasn't doing this in an aggressive manner, I knew we couldn't let her continue to "talk" with her teeth. This was another problematic behavior we needed to stop.

"No, LaRoux," she would hear. "We don't put our teeth on people." We figured she didn't understand our words but hoped the tone in our voices conveyed the message. We also stopped playing with her when this happened. Sadly, the "teeth on people" issue continued with no change in her behavior.

Our immediate response in both these situations was to punish LaRoux. Accidents in the house? Take her outside. Putting her teeth on people? No more playing. Though these strategies sometimes successfully stopped behaviors in the short term, they weren't eliminating them for good.

While driving LaRoux to puppy training one day, I remember thinking about these specific problem behaviors and wondering, *When will LaRoux learn?* As I quickly discovered in the class that followed, my thought process should have been different. The real question I should have asked myself was, *When will LaRoux's dad learn?*

As soon as LaRoux entered the training area of her class, she ran up to one of her friends, a giant Labrador retriever, and left a puddle right next to him. Then, she greeted the lab's owner by gently putting her teeth on the lady's hand. "Welcome to the world of the excited young puppy," the trainer said as she went to get a paper towel to clean up the mess.

As I pulled LaRoux away to take her to her spot, the lightbulb in my head finally turned on. LaRoux's behaviors were not conscious responses or choices but emotional reactions triggered by the surrounding environment. This is why punishment wasn't working. Rather than focusing on LaRoux's behaviors, I needed to focus on managing her emotional state through the environment. LaRoux needed grounding.

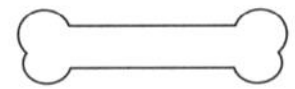

Our surroundings matter. When walking into a room full of people, we can immediately feel the emotional climate without anyone saying a word. And this emotional climate can have a substantial impact on our emotional states. Put another way—emotions feed emotions.

Kids are significantly impacted by their surroundings because regions of their brains that regulate their emotions are not yet well developed. Rather than managing and guiding their feelings internally, they often take cues from external stimuli. For this reason, adults need to be aware of the environment kids are exposed to so we don't inadvertently escalate behaviors in the process.

MANAGING THE ENVIRONMENT

Overstimulation—that was the reason LaRoux put her teeth on people and had potty accidents. She got excited, and the emotional parts of her brain overrode the cognitive structures needed to make good choices. She was reacting to her emotions rather than being able to respond to them.

This often happens to young children when they are playing together. They "ramp up" quickly but have a more difficult time calming down. Their young development impacts this, but it is also because they feed off each other's heightened emotional states. So, rather than working with young developing brains to make better choices when overstimulated, the first response should be altering the environmental factors that trigger their behaviors.

When children are in a heightened emotional state, their brains are less likely to process spoken information than react to emotional cues.

Our Behaviors

Ever play the game "Follow the Leader?" This game serves as a great reminder that kids will follow our lead. So, we need to be intentional about modeling calm behaviors. When children are in a heightened emotional state, their brains are less likely to process spoken information than react to emotional cues. This makes our emotional demeanor very important.

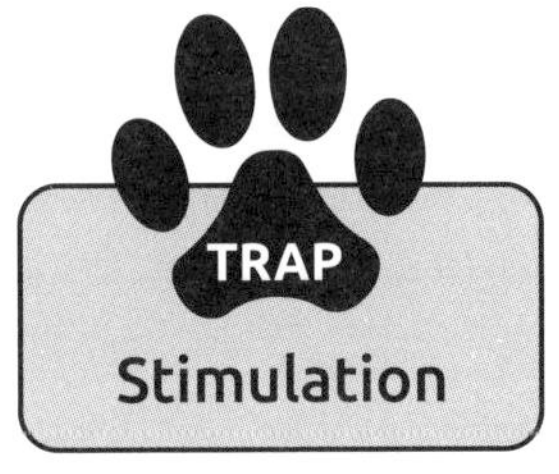

Knowing that children feed off our emotional states, it is essential for adults not to inadvertently overstimulate children with our emotional states, be that excitement or frustration. Though adults can more quickly calm down once stimulated, this process takes longer for young developing brains.

The Behavior of Others

Divide and conquer—it's a simple yet often underutilized strategy. Just as children feed off our emotional state, so do they react to the emotions and behaviors of others. Accordingly, removing the audience is a very effective strategy for helping a child stay calm and grounded.

When we get a child alone, we eliminate a great deal of external stimulation, which can quickly change the emotional temperature of a situation. And as any teacher can confirm, children respond differently to us when peers are not around. When we speak with children alone, we can also better influence their behavior because they don't have to divide their focus among people.

The Physical Environment

Just as a person's emotional state can cause overstimulation, so can our surroundings. Have you ever walked into a messy space and had an overwhelming urge to straighten it? A friend's house? A fellow teacher's desk? This compulsion comes from our need for order. Whereas clutter can create chaos, clean and orderly environments can create calm. This does not mean we need sterile, minimalist spaces for our kids, but we should be aware of the physical environment so as not to overstimulate inadvertently.

Just as a person's emotional state can cause overstimulation, so can our surroundings.

DIRECT INSTRUCTION

Though managing the environment is essential in helping ground children emotionally, our ultimate goal is to help them recognize their feelings and self-regulate. When doing so, we must remember that the younger children are, the less practice they have had dealing with their emotions. So just as with any other skill, kids need to be explicitly taught when it comes to managing their emotional states.

...just as with any other skill, kids need to be explicitly taught when it comes to managing their emotional states.

Identifying Feelings

The first step in dealing with our feelings is recognizing and labeling them. We can help teach children this skill through language modeling:

> *"Mrs. Johnson's feeling sad this morning."*
> *"Tyrone, you look excited about going to the park."*
> *"Rascal's shaking in her cage. She looks scared."*

When labeling the feelings, we also have an excellent opportunity to expose kids to rich language by continuously varying our word choice:

> *"Mrs. Johnson's feeling* ***down*** *this morning."*
> *"Tyrone, you look* ***enthusiastic*** *about going to the park."*
> *"Rascal's shaking in her cage. She looks* ***frightened****."*

We also learn how to identify feelings through seeing the facial expressions of others. In addition to modeling different emotions to kids, we should be providing them with ample interaction time with their peers. Increased face-to-face time gives the brain more opportunities to learn how to identify feelings in others.

In the classroom setting, labeling feelings can be a great morning ritual. Teachers can make a feelings wall with pictures of kids expressing different emotions. As students enter the classroom each morning, they are encouraged to put a clothespin with their name next to the emotion they are feeling.

Expressing Feelings

Once we learn to identify our feelings, we must learn to manage and express them appropriately. This skill can also be taught through language modeling:

> *"When Mrs. Judson is confused, it helps when she talks through things. Let's all come to the carpet."*
> *"Mom is feeling tired. She's going to rest for a little while."*

This skill can also be taught through direct instruction. It's important to teach a variety of strategies, so children have options and can choose what works best for them. For example,

- Going to a calming area of the room
- Listening to music in a center
- Looking at a book
- Jumping on the class trampoline

No matter the strategy used, it is important to work with kids on expressing their feelings with their words. I love to use animals as a concrete way to help kids understand talking about their feelings:

> *"When LaRoux gets scared, she barks loudly. She can't talk, so that's her way of telling us how she's feeling. We are lucky that we can use our words."*

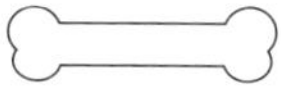

The happy ending to this chapter is that LaRoux's potty accidents, for the most part, have stopped. She's also gotten much better about not "grabbing" people with her mouth. We believe this is because she has gotten older and has better impulse control. Another factor in her success is that her owners do a much better job fulfilling her need for emotional grounding.

Prior to LaRoux meeting new people, we get her alone, use a calm voice, remove distractions like toys, and focus her attention. By settling her proactively, we know we are increasing the likelihood she will be more successful in a new social setting.

LESSON LEARNED

Emotions feed emotions.

Kids need to feel emotionally grounded. When they do, they feel safe—which positively impacts their feelings and, ultimately, their behaviors. Adults can help meet this need by modeling, managing the environment, and providing kids with direct instruction on how best to self-regulate their emotional states.

CHAPTER TWO

BOUNDARIES

LaRoux is food motivated. We discovered this the first time we fed her alongside our other two dogs. Each dog had a bowl of food in separate areas of the kitchen; however, LaRoux tried to claim all three. We thought our other dogs would defend their food and territories, providing LaRoux with natural consequences, but this did not happen. The other two dogs took a passive role, stepped back, and kindly deferred to her.

As my wife and I watched LaRoux guard the three bowls, she seemed to be working herself up into a frenzy. Her anxiety increased, and her behaviors became more erratic. She ran from bowl to bowl, and if one of the other dogs so much as looked too closely at a bowl, LaRoux would let out a warning bark. Something had to change. We needed to intervene if our other dogs ever stood a chance of getting to eat.

We started by giving LaRoux her food and letting her begin to eat before pouring food into the other dogs' bowls. We also stood guard. If LaRoux went toward the other bowls, we redirected her to her own. At first, we had to physically stand between her and her siblings' food for this to be successful. However, with continued coaching and support, LaRoux eventually accepted that she could only eat the food in her bowl.

Like a kid in a candy shop, LaRoux *wanted* all the food, but she *needed* to be given boundaries.

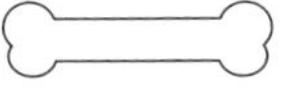

Let's face it; young children aren't the best self-managers. If left alone with cookies, most kids will eat too many—and feel sick. If given a video game before bed, many kids will stay up too late playing it—and feel tired the following day. This is because young children focus on what's right in front of them rather than thinking ahead. They live in the moment, striving to get their immediate needs met, not seeing the potential consequences of their choices.

It's a brain-development thing. Actually, it's a lack-of-brain-development thing. The frontal lobes, responsible for more advanced cognitive functions such as self-control and judgment, are not strongly developed in young brains. So, the emotional impulsivity of *"I want this now"* precedes the cognitive reasoning of *"This probably isn't best for me."*

Generally, the younger the brain is, the more external help it needs to make good choices. This is why children need to be given limits by adults. Limits help kids not only stay safe but feel safe. When we know the boundaries, our anxiety decreases.

...the younger the brain is, the more external help it needs to make good choices.

Children who aren't given boundaries are at risk of becoming selfish, focusing mainly on their wants and needs. This creates social skills problems when interacting with their peers. Lack of boundaries can also lead to a sense of entitlement and children being conditioned for immediate gratification. Both of these issues have a negative impact on emotional and social development.

Our ultimate goal in giving children limits is that they learn to provide self-imposed boundaries when they are older. This is why adults must enforce limits persistently. Consistent external limits get kids to learn how to live within them.

Boundaries also help children practice accepting disappointment, a critical behavioral skill they must learn. If kids can't handle minor disappointments when young, they will have

If kids can't handle minor disappointments when young, they will have difficulty managing the major ones they will inevitably face when older.

difficulty managing the major ones they will inevitably face when older. No matter our age, we don't always get what we want.

One of the best ways to help kids practice accepting boundaries is to provide limits by telling children "no" when warranted. This helps children learn to regulate their emotional states and appropriately handle frustration and disappointment. There are simple strategies adults can use to help kids accept boundaries:

- Pre-teach the expectation that sometimes adults have to tell children "no." Hearing this at a neutral time is easier for children to understand and accept rather than processing the information when a boundary is established.
- Give kids logical rationales for why they are not getting what they want. (e.g., *"That tree has skinny branches. It wouldn't be safe to climb."*)
- Defer to a later time when the child *might* receive "yes" as an answer. (e.g., *"We might get ice cream tomorrow—but not right now, since we're about to eat lunch."*)
- Model accepting "no" for an answer appropriately. By doing so, we show empathy. (e.g., *"Ms. Fiona's upset right now. I wanted our class to go outside, but we can't because it's raining. We'll have fun inside instead."*)

Some adults struggle to provide boundaries and tell children "no." This is often the case with teachers and parents whose children exhibit more severe behaviors. The adults raise their tolerance level to avoid having power struggles.

"If I don't let him play on my phone, he throws a fit. I give him the phone to keep peace in the family."

"Penny, we talked about this yesterday. I said you wouldn't get to go to the next center today if you didn't clean up the first one. I'll let you go, but you need to clean it up tomorrow."

Allowing kids to have what they want might ward off immediate temper tantrums. Still, it also creates a more prominent issue moving forward—children who have difficulty accepting limits as they age. And the longer this pattern continues, the harder it will be for them to deal with boundaries they will inevitably face.

I'm often asked about boundary issues with parents who have divorced. "I provide limits when my child is with me, but his father doesn't. My son tells me he can watch movies and stay up late at his dad's. I don't know how to handle that. I look like the mean parent when trying to do the right thing."

When able, we want to work with other adults to provide consistent boundaries so children receive unified messages about expectations. However, when this is not happening, there are several things to keep in mind:

- Focus on what you can control, which are the expectations in your environment: "Remember, Michelle, sometimes adults handle things differently. We can look at books at mom's house before bed, but no electronics."
- Reinforce reasons for expectations: "Going to bed now gives us a good, full night's sleep. When we go to bed late, our bodies don't get enough rest."

- Once you provide a boundary and rationale, don't belabor the point by continuously repeating yourself. The more we talk, the more the discussion can move from expectation to negotiation.
- Remember that as adults, we are first and foremost role models. Refrain from speaking negatively about other adults to or in front of children. Adults may not always agree, but we must do so in ways that do not inadvertently teach our children judgment and poor verbal impulse control.

The good news is that developing brains learn to adapt and adjust to different individuals and environments. Once boundaries are established with one adult, a child will most likely learn to accept them, regardless of other adult interactions.

Just as it is beneficial for kids to have the opportunity to connect with a diverse group of peers, so it is good for them to interact with a diverse array of adults. Children respond differently to different adults, so the more kids are given appropriate direction and boundaries by adults other than their parents, the more likely they will be to apply these skills to other settings.

When children are given limits, it is natural for them to push back and test them. Their brain's irrational, emotional areas often override the cognitive ones, which can result in the less-than-desirable behaviors of name-calling and fit-throwing. These behaviors, though unpleasant, are normal and should be expected.

Adults need to practice staying calm and modeling good composure when this happens. Not only does this help de-escalate the situation and avoid potential power struggles, but it also teaches children how to stay emotionally grounded when frustrated, as noted in the last chapter.

LESSON LEARNED

Defined limits help us feel safe.

When children aren't given healthy boundaries, they often push the limits of behaviors. When clearly identified and applied, boundaries teach children critical life skills they will need as they age, including responsibility, respect, self-discipline, and resourcefulness.

CHAPTER THREE

CONSISTENCY

Trying to teach puppies to refrain from jumping on people is a challenging task for many reasons:

- They naturally want to get as close to people as possible because of their desire for connection and affection.
- Young brains are self-focused, so they don't read social cues well (meaning they have little awareness of how their behaviors are being received by the people getting jumped on).
- Impulse control is hard for the developing brain. Puppies are bombarded with an abundance of joy when they see people. This triggers the *reaction* of jumping rather than the *response* of waiting to be petted.

- They have not learned or practiced how to greet people appropriately.
- They get confused because they receive mixed messages about what they are supposed to do when people approach.

Have you ever seen a young child greet a puppy? It's like two parallel Disneyland worlds colliding. The child is excited to see the puppy, the puppy is excited to see the child, and the result is a dog overtaken by tail-wagging, running in circles, licking, and, naturally, constant jumping.

Though I don't have young children anymore, this example is what it felt like every time LaRoux approached my wife or older sons. Being the stern disciplinarian of the family, I would intervene to create a teachable moment. "Wait! Make her sit down and settle before you pet her," I would say. "But she's adorable!" they would reply…as she jumped up on them… and they petted her…and smiled. Of course, the problem was that every time someone would smile or pet her, LaRoux was encouraged, so the jumping-on-people behavior continued.

I would love to be the hero of this story, indicating that I, and I alone, broke the cycle of mixed messages LaRoux was receiving—and consistently enforced the expectation that she sit before being petted. But alas, that would be a lie.

In reality, LaRoux wore me down. After a long day, I'd come home to her excited, cute puppy face. She would jump up, and before my brain remembered to enforce sitting and settling, I would smile and pet LaRoux—further engraining the poor behavior into a habit.

If we were ever to change her habit of jumping, we needed to provide consistency when trying to enforce our behavioral expectations.

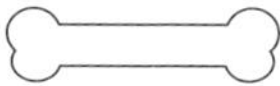

"The only person who likes change is a baby with a wet diaper." Thank you, Mark Twain. Change is hard. We prefer consistency. We don't have to think as hard when things are the same. Knowing what is to come allows us to delegate many behaviors to automation. This means our anxiety is lowered, and we can relax.

However, when we encounter something different, our brains must, to some degree, stay alert, process the new information, and decide how to respond.

There is a stoplight close to your house. Every morning you back out of your driveway, pull up to the light, and take action. If the signal is red, you stop; green, you go. Most mornings, you aren't even aware you are doing this. It's an automated routine.

One morning you wake up after a terrible storm, approach the light, and discover it is neither red nor green; it is out. You and the other drivers slow down as you drive to the intersection. Everyone is scanning the area, trying to anticipate the actions of other drivers and, accordingly, decide how to proceed. Albeit ever so slightly, tensions are raised.

Parents of very young children experience this type of difficulty with change when bedtime routines are disrupted. Teachers experience it when daily schedules are altered. Adults and children experienced it on a large scale when we were introduced to the Coronavirus. During the pandemic, everything changed. *Everyone was at the intersection, but the stoplight wasn't working.*

Though the onset of the pandemic was quite some time ago, residual anxiety from all the changes encountered continues to linger. The tension can be felt with adults and is often evidenced by their behaviors. Fortunately, young brains are malleable, so if we provide consistency in their lives, we can lower children's anxiety brought on by changes around them.

Teachers know firsthand the importance of being consistent in the classroom. Classes with solid routines and consistently followed procedures flow better and have fewer behavioral interruptions than those that don't. Enforcing consistency in the classroom usually gets more manageable as students age since their development impacts this issue.

Classes with solid routines and consistently followed procedures flow better and have fewer behavioral interruptions than those that don't.

"I can't figure out why I'm struggling with my class this year," a teacher once told me. "For some reason, I'm dealing with many behavior issues." I asked her to give me a few specific examples, and she provided three:

- "They interrupt and shout out while I'm reading stories. It's hard for me to make it through one story without interruptions."
- "They don't follow directions when transitioning to recess, so we are late almost every day."
- "They are very quick to tattle when other kids in the room do something wrong."

I went to her class for a brief observation and quickly discovered the issue. It seems the problem was one of consistency. She had expectations in place for each of these concerns:

- Wait until after a story to ask questions. If it's an emergency, raise a hand quietly.
- When putting jackets on to go to recess, try to zip and button them yourselves. Ask for help from friends when needed.
- When you have a problem with someone, use your words to solve it.

Though these expectations were in place, the teacher intermittently enforced them:

- When children shouted out or raised their hands (with non-emergencies) during stories, the teacher sometimes acknowledged students before redirecting them.
- Most students put on their jackets and went straight to the teacher for help with buttoning and zipping.
- When children "tattled," the teacher would respond by redirecting the reported student and, at times, reminding the "tattler" of the expectation to use their own words to try to solve the problem.

"I don't understand," the teacher said. "I'm a person who loves routine. Outside the classroom, every part of my world is consistent, planned, and scheduled. Why is it so hard to be consistent with my students?" The probable answer had to do with developing brains and their inclination toward impulsivity.

This problem is common for adults working with children—especially younger kids. To be consistent, we must first develop and teach an expectation, then respond when it is or is not followed. Adults often do a great job with the planning part of this equation. The follow-through, however, is the challenge.

Adult expectations and plans are usually based on *responses*. However, young brains quickly pull us into the world of *reactions*. Many of the children's behavior concerns we deal with are impulsive, coming from an emotional place. The timing of these behaviors (while everyone is excited about a story, going outside, or upset with another friend in the class) often catches us off guard, so rather than consistently responding and redirecting, we impulsively react (by answering, zipping, or solving).

A great starting place for providing consistency is by having solid routines and expectations for children to follow that are conveyed with consistent language phrases:

Getting Attention:	*"One, two, three…eyes on me."*
Transitions:	*"Time to line up at the door, walking safely 'cross the floor."*
Bedtime 4 'B' Ritual:	*"Brush, Bath, Book, and Bed"* (*Brush* our teeth. Take a *bath*. Read a *book*. Go to *bed*.)

When kids hear these short, directional phrases, we meet their need for clarity by reducing confusion. Their repetitive nature builds strong patterns of understanding, helping them better anticipate what is to come. This pairing both lowers their anxiety and strengthens the likelihood that positive behaviors will follow.

Consistency can be easier to follow when we are all working together. When developing classroom or home routines, involve children in the process. This gives them a sense of ownership in the practices while helping meet their need for control.

Teachers can evaluate the consistency of their classroom routines by simply being absent. In classrooms with consistent schedules and expectations, children know what to do in the teacher's absence and need little guidance. In classrooms where procedures and expectations are not consistently followed, the students look to the substitute teacher for continual guidance.

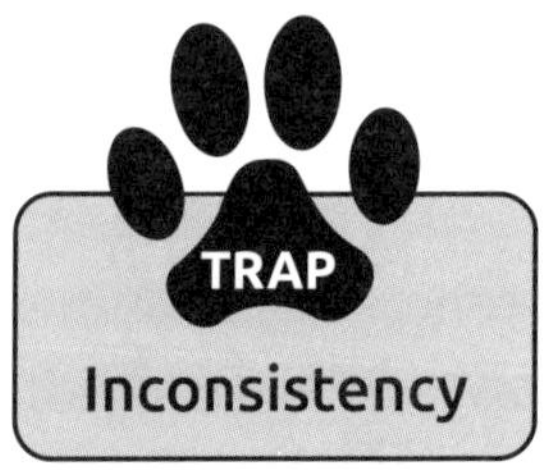

Adults must be careful not to send mixed messages to children by having expectations and not following them. For example, expecting that hands are raised to get attention—and then calling on students who shout out. If we have expectations, we need to consistently follow them to the extent possible.

LESSON LEARNED

Anxiety is lowered when we can anticipate what is to come.

Consistency develops healthy patterns in the brain that help kids feel safe and secure in their environment. And the more change children experience in certain areas, the stronger a positive impact adults can make by providing consistency in other ways.

CHAPTER FOUR

CLARITY

When LaRoux attended her first beginner puppy class, we were excited to discover she was a quick learner. She picked up basic directions such as *sit, down, shake,* and *kennel* with no problem. By the end of the sessions, she easily earned her beginner's puppy-training certificate. However, things got more challenging in the intermediate class. She often got confused—*shaking* when prompted to *salute, lying down* when prompted to *relax,* and going to her *kennel* when directed to go to her *mat.* Though it was understandable why she would get confused, both dog and owner got frustrated when it occurred.

When LaRoux started her third class, I realized she was getting overwhelmed. Her brain was trying to process all the skills she had learned previously while also trying to take in new skills. This often put her over the edge. Usually, by the end of a class, when I gave LaRoux a direction, she would throw out many behaviors to see if any seemed correct. She'd sit, then wave, then run to her kennel. When I looked at her expression, it was as if she was screaming, *"I give up! What do you want from me?"*

If I didn't give her a break, LaRoux would often self-select one by running around the training area, picking up toys, or jumping on me. I was able to adjust my perspective and understand she wasn't exhibiting these behaviors out of defiance. Behavior is communication. She was simply trying to tell me, "I'm confused—and I'm done."

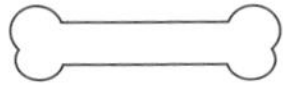

Most teachers of young children can relate to at least one version of this scenario:

Version 1—Nothing

Mr. Saucedo asks his students, "Who knows what day it is? We've been talking about this for a while. It's a special one." Half the kids in the class raise their hands, hoping to get the chance to answer. Bethany is called on. Silence. Bethany is prompted. Bethany smiles and timidly puts her hand down. Mr. Saucedo turns to another child with a raised hand—and the sequence of events repeats itself.

Version 2—Somewhat Related

Mrs. Gurwitz finishes reading a book to her class. "What a fun book that was! Now, can anyone tell me the dog's name in this story? It's so silly!" Eager hands are raised, and Mrs. Gurwitz calls on a student. "Yes, Jason?" "We have a dog," he calls out, "and one of his eyes doesn't open all the way. My dad said it's tired. I get tired sometimes too."

Version 3—Not Even Close

Mrs. Pena has just started circle time with her students and directs their attention to the job chart. "I wonder," she says. "Does anyone remember who our line leader was yesterday? I'm not sure." Michael raises his hand and is called on. "My mom got her hair cut, and it looks like yours!"

In all three of these examples, it is not uncommon for several children to be called on before finding one who has an answer to the specific question asked.

"I remind the kids to listen carefully to the questions I'm asking," explains one teacher, "but they don't pay attention." "I tell them to make sure they have an answer in their heads before raising a hand," another teacher tells me, "but they have a hard time following directions."

Following directions is an essential skill for our kids to learn. However, to do so, they must not only pay attention but also sustain attention. This is hard for young children because their developing brains have small short-term memory capacities. Instead of maintaining attention, kids fall prey to *Squirrel Syndrome*, attending to whatever shiny object catches their eyes.

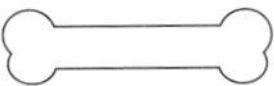

One of the best ways to help kids deal with this issue is through clarity when communicating. Since kids have difficulty keeping information in short-term memory, we must be intentional about how and how much of it we throw at them at once.

"Alright, friends," said Mrs. Schwab, "it's almost time to go out to recess, but remember, when you line up, you will need to get your jacket. It's cold outside, and we don't want anyone getting sick. So, finish up your project and start cleaning your area."

This is an excellent example of how well-intentioned teachers can give too much information to children simultaneously. And when this happens, the likelihood that children understand and follow our directions is minimal.

A good way to begin providing kids with greater clarity is by adopting the practice of Economy of Language. This is a theory of using a few very specific words when communicating. The idea is that the information we convey is better understood by eliminating redundant or unnecessary words and phrases in our speech. Economy of Language is helpful to use when giving children directions.

EFFECTIVE DIRECTION GIVING

<u>Step #1</u> in giving kids directions is getting their attention. The brain can only consciously attend to one thing at a time, so if

we want kids to follow our directions, we must secure their attention first.

Step #2 is giving directions in small chunks. Give one or two short directions using an Economy of Language approach before providing additional ones. Say what you need to say in as few words as possible, starting the direction with a verb or noun.

Verbs	Nouns
"***Push*** in your chair."	"***Eyes*** on me."
"***Get*** your backpack."	"***Hands*** in our laps."
"***Find*** your spot."	"***Shoes*** by the door."

Starting a direction with a verb immediately calls the brain to action. The verb focuses the brain on a specific outcome and gives it a mental picture of what to do. Nouns are another way to provide the brain with an internal visual, helping kids see where we want their focus.

Starting a direction with a verb immediately calls the brain to action.

Consider using external visuals as well. Holding up or pointing to an object, using a specific gesture, or providing parallel assistance by modeling the direction are all ways to strengthen our message,

Step #3 is providing wait time for the direction to be followed. The brain needs time to process the information. Wait time increases the likelihood that kids will successfully carry out the directions.

- "Get your jacket..."
- "Finish that thought..."
- "Put books in the bin..."

Not securing children's attention before giving directions:

If kids are not paying attention when we start giving directions, they miss out on part of the information. This decreases the likelihood they will follow them. (This is especially true if you start the direction with an action verb, which is the most important word!) Additionally, when we talk over children, we are setting the expectation that it is okay to talk while directions are being given.

Using too many unnecessary words and phrases:

This is the most common trap for most adults. The more words we throw into directions, the more kids must fish out the verbs to follow them. Three phrases are consistent traps for adults:

- "Alright, kids, in a minute, **I want you to...**"
- "Right now, **I need you to...**"
- "Guys, in a little while, **I'm going to ask you to...**"

Avoid this specific trap by starting with the verb!

- "Alright, kids, **get** your coats**...**"
- "Right now, **move** to the next center..."
- "Guys, **line up** for lunch**...**"

Giving too many directions at once:

When we provide single-step directions for young kids, we increase the likelihood they will be successful in following them. As they get older and their short-term memory storage becomes larger, they will be in a better position to follow multi-step directions successfully.

But at our school, students are expected to follow multi-step directions. How do I handle this?

This is a common expectation in many early childhood classrooms. The way to build kids' ability to follow multi-step directions is to find places in their routine where you can provide the same set of directions daily. When children repeatedly hear the same multi-step directions, the brain processes the information as one direction, connected by three small steps. For example,

- "Push in chairs, get your jackets, and line up."
- "Wash your hands, get a drink, and come to the carpet."
- "Find your folder, look at the chart, and head to your center."

When given too much information, kids' brains short-circuit.

Information overload can overwhelm us all, but this is especially true for young children. When given too much information, kids' brains short-circuit. At best, this leads to confusion, and at worst, this leads to silly and disruptive behaviors.

We can combat this problem by slowing down, practicing Economy of Language, and chunking directions and other information we give kids. This one takes time to master, but the outcome is more than worth the investment.

LESSON LEARNED

Confusion can easily lead to misbehavior.

The more adults can help children understand expectations through clear language and action, the greater the positive outcomes. We must remember that the developing brain can only hold so much information in immediate and short-term memory and consider this when communicating.

CHAPTER FIVE

JOY

I can't explain why, but I feel certain there is a magical magnetic force between dogs and socks—and LaRoux always got caught up in it. Every time we washed a load of laundry, the same frustrating routine would play out.

The *fun* started after taking clothes out of the dryer. Because we were aware of LaRoux's inclination to collect items, I always looked around my feet to make sure I had not dropped anything before proceeding. (I also double-checked to be sure our cat had not jumped into the warm dryer, which he often did.)

With a clean floor at my feet and warm clothes pressed against my chest, I walked to the couch, dropped the laundry, and proceeded to fold. I never figured out how it happened almost every time—but like clockwork, LaRoux would appear behind the couch with one of my clean socks in her mouth.

"LaRoux! Drop that," I would tell her. In response, her reaction was to take off running, and mine was to follow. It usually took a while, but inevitably, after a bit of darting around, I would catch up with her. "Drop it," I would say again, using my commanding bass *"I mean it"* voice. However, that didn't work most of the time, so I'd have to pry her mouth open to get my sock back. She always looked so sad afterward.

One day after witnessing one of these incidents, my wife looked at me and said, "Well, you're no fun." And that's when it dawned on me. LaRoux just wanted to play, and I was the mean daddy telling her playtime was over. To change LaRoux's behavior, I had to find a way to infuse play into the equation. A few days later, another opportunity presented itself.

On cue, LaRoux ran up to me with a sock in her mouth. This time, rather than chasing and scolding, I clapped my hands. "Good girl!" I said as I ran from LaRoux into the kitchen where her toys were. LaRoux followed my lead and ran toward me. "You got a sock," I said in a cheerful voice. "I'm so proud of you. Let's play!" And as I sat down on the floor and picked up

LaRoux's favorite brown bear, she jumped into my lap and dropped the sock.

As soon as the sock left her mouth, I threw her brown bear across the room. In doing so, I changed our game from *chase* to *fetch*. And just like that, the problem was solved.

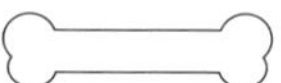

When I ask adults what they love about children, three words frequently pop up: *funny, happy,* and *innocent*. This usually leads us to a larger discussion about specific children and sharing stories that reflect these traits.

I recall reading a story to a group of kindergarten students and being so impressed with the boy right in front of me who was intently focused throughout the entire book. Having a history with this child and knowing his difficulty paying attention, I was pleased. *We are definitely making progress with him,* I thought.

The child's hand shot up as soon as I finished reading the story. Wanting to validate his excellent behavior and hear about his takeaway from the book, I called on him. "Mr. St. Romain!" he said, giggling, "you have a huge booger in your nose!" At this point, I glanced up at the boy's teacher. She smiled, let out an audible laugh, and mumbled under her breath, "Ah, the joy of early childhood."

It doesn't take a lot. Children can notice the slightest thing and find joy and wonder in it. Since joy is based in positive emotions, and wonder is based in curiosity, it's easy to understand why these traits are natural and healthy expressions for the developing brain.

When the brain is young and growing, pathways are created that shape development. Positive emotional states, such as joy, produce pathways that encourage future healthy emotions and behaviors. They also allow healthy *responsive* pathways to be formed to regions of the brain responsible for reasoning, cause-and-effect, and problem-solving.

Negative emotional states like fear and anger develop *reactive* brain pathways. Intense or frequent negative emotions often trigger children to impulsively move into fight, flight, or freeze mode. All three of these reactions somewhat limit access to responsive pathways.

The big idea here? The brain pathways that are the strongest are the ones most likely to be used. So, the more we can encourage positive emotional states in children, the more we are laying the groundwork for healthy emotional regulation as they age. This has huge implications for how we interact with kids, especially when dealing with discipline issues.

...the more we can encourage positive emotional states in children, the more we are laying the groundwork for healthy emotional regulation as they age.

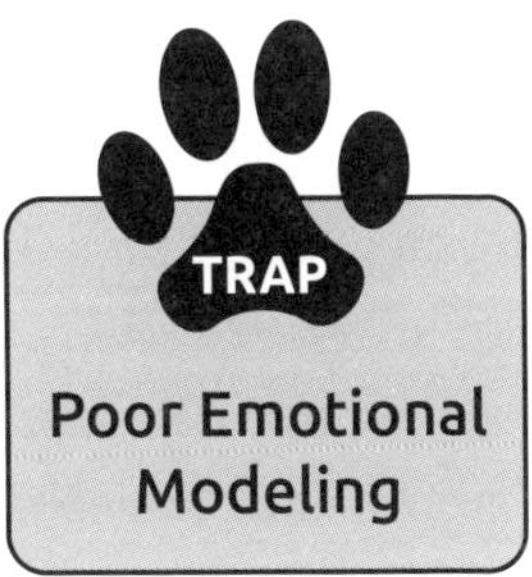

Fear can cause the developing brain to shut down, so adults should be careful to take an appropriate tone when disciplining children. Yelling and modeling out-of-control emotional states through our words and actions work against our ultimate efforts to positively shape our children's behaviors.

"He needs to make a better choice." I hear this phrase often from adults when behavior issues arise. If we want children to make choices, we need to make sure our interactions with them keep them in healthy emotional states of *responding* rather than in fearful or defensive emotional states of impulsively *reacting.* One of the best ways to do this is to build on their natural state of joy.

Fortunately, children often toggle between emotional states relatively easily. They can be furious one minute, storming out of a room, and return happy and laughing the next minute, as though nothing ever happened to upset them. This occurs because children have limited attention spans, and the brain can only consciously focus on one thing at a time.

Because children are easily distracted, we can use this as a strategy to avoid getting into power struggles with them. The best way to do so is by directing attention away from concerns and creating opportunities for joyful experiences. Here are two examples:

Mrs. Hargrove sings a song, signaling the end of center time. *"It's time to come to the carpet. It's time, don't wait. Come and see…"* By the time the song ends, all the children are on the carpet except Malachi, who is arranging magnetic letters on a cookie sheet. Mrs. Hargrove prompts Malachi, but he continues to work with the letters. "I wonder who can guess what's in my mystery bag this morning. You can ask me questions," says Mrs. Hargrove excitedly. Malachi looks at the bag and then back at the letters. Wilma raises her hand. "What color is it?" she asks. "It's red. Just like the color of one boy's shoes in this room!" Mrs. Hargrove says, smiling. Malachi looks at the bag, then looks at his shoes. "Is it a toy?" Molly asks. "No, but it is something you can eat. In fact, someone in this room brings one to lunch every day!" says Mrs. Hargrove. Malachi smiles, runs to the carpet, and raises his hand. "Is it an apple?" he asks. "Why, yes. Malachi. That is exactly what's in my bag!" Mrs. Hargrove says.

James and his mom go shopping for groceries. James grabs a bag of gummy worms as they pass by a counter on the way into the store. Mom tells James she is not purchasing the gummy worms but that he can help pick out a different dessert to eat after lunch. James holds the gummy worms tight against his chest. "Let's see," says mom. "What should we have for lunch when we get home? Pickled Brussels sprouts and liver, or macaroni and cheese?" she asks. James smiles. "Mac and cheese!" he says. "That works for me," she says. "Will you grab that box and put it in our cart for mom?" James sets the gummy worms down in the cart and gets the box of macaroni and cheese. As they walk through the store, mom directs James' attention to foods he likes and away from the gummy worms. When they get to the baking section, she helps James pick a brownie mix. "Great choice," she says. "Let's have brownies for dessert." She hands him the brownie box and puts the gummy worms on the shelf.

The goal is to keep the focus away from misbehavior and increase positive emotions around the desired behaviors.

In these examples, behavioral boundaries were provided but done so in ways that build on the natural joy inherent in children. The goal is to keep the focus away from misbehavior and increase positive emotions around the desired behaviors. This approach may not always work, but it is an excellent first step when trying to positively shape behaviors in children.

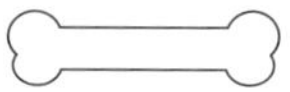

As Mary Poppins so eloquently put it, *"In every job that must be done, there is an element of fun."* And any time adults can find fun by infusing joy into the equation, we connect with children in a developmentally appropriate place. Whether the goal is to get kids to clean up, learn a new skill, or just come to the table to eat, motivation increases when a task is rooted in a positive emotional state.

LESSON LEARNED

Fun is one of the best natural motivators.

Often, our interactions inadvertently put children in emotional distress, which triggers disruptive behaviors. The brain is survival-oriented and does not like being in this state of distress. When we infuse joy into our interactions with kids, we draw on their natural desire to be in positive emotional states, which leads to positive outcomes concerning their behaviors.

CHAPTER SIX

BELONGING

The timing couldn't have been worse. It was Thanksgiving Day, and we had about twenty people en route to our house for a family feast. The last thing I planned was to chase our four-legged furry beasts around the neighborhood. But that's what happened.

The fun started when Odin, LaRoux's older brother, slipped out of an open door. Odin is a gentle, giant husky with one problematic behavior: he's a runner. When he gets loose, he's gone. (Truth be known, that is how we probably came to have him as a family member. We feel sure he had run away from his home of origin, ending up in our care.) As soon as Odin shot out of the house, LaRoux followed him. And thus, the game began.

We called the dogs, knowing Odin would not likely heed our call, but we were hopeful LaRoux would be led by her conscience and return to us. This didn't happen—at first. Wherever Odin went, LaRoux followed in hot pursuit.

They shot around the nearby yards before dashing around the corner beyond my sight. When I realized their return was not imminent, I jumped into my car to find them. Fortunately, I only made it halfway down the street when I saw LaRoux heading back my way. As soon as I opened the car door, she jumped in, and I breathed a sigh of relief.

As she looked at me with her "That was so much fun!" face, I imagined a giant speech bubble floating above her head, saying, "Dad. Odin ran far. We're not supposed to do that. Are we?" I choose to think LaRoux's ethical conscience finally kicked in. It just took a little more time to do so than I would have hoped.

After we got both dogs back to the house, I had some reflection time and realized the problem. Initially, LaRoux had to choose between following her brother or following me. And given those options, her need to belong was overriding her motivation to follow directions.

For both dogs, this activity met several needs—all of which were working against me. They were getting to run *(need for physical activity)*, having fun *(need for joy)*, and spending time together *(need for belonging)*. Is it any wonder why my one adult-centered *need for control* was not getting met?

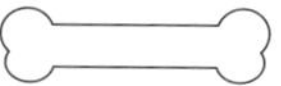

The *Circle of Courage* is a model based on Native American child-rearing practices highlighting four assets needed for healthy development: Belonging, Mastery, Generosity, and Independence. Each trait builds a sense of resilience in children, contributing to a healthy self-concept.

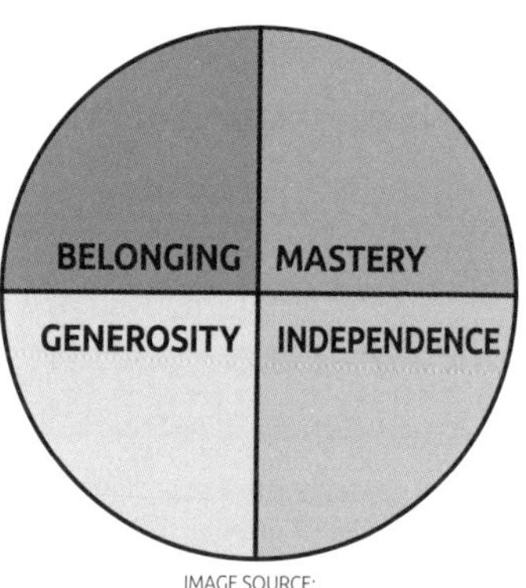

IMAGE SOURCE:
HTTPS://EN.WIKIPEDIA.ORG/WIKI/CIRCLE_OF_COURAGE

Belonging is the foundation of this model. It highlights our need for attachment which starts at birth. From the time babies are born, they are dependent on others for survival. Their connection with caregivers forms the first building blocks of meeting their need to belong. The more trusting and positive these connections, the healthier the child's development.

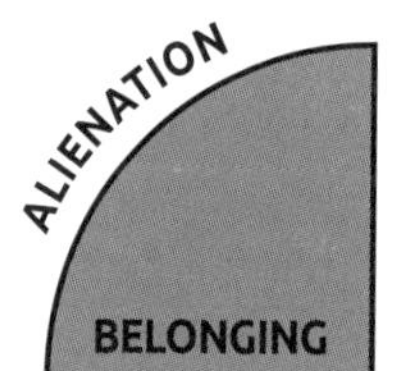

If the need to belong is not met, children will have difficulty developing the other three traits of Mastery, Generosity, and Independence. Children who don't form secure bonds with others are prone to experience isolation, which can lead to alienation and anti-social behaviors. Children who don't connect with others also don't develop a sense of trust for others or the environment. When this happens, children are left trying to get their need for belonging met in unhealthy ways.

As children grow and move through various stages of development, they form different types of connections, which help them relate to others and strengthen their sense of belonging. Babies, for example, will mimic facial expressions. Toddlers will toddle, following a parent around the room.

Children who don't form secure bonds with others are prone to experience isolation, which can lead to alienation and anti-social behaviors.

Young children's sense of belonging is survival-based because they depend on others to meet their needs. Though young children are egocentric, their language often highlights an attempt to connect with others.

- "I need help!"
- "Look at me!"
- "I want one!!"

At around five years of age, children move into a stage of development characterized strongly by awareness of others and their relationship with them. Their attempt to belong can be heard through their interactions with other children.

- "You can play with us!"
- "Will you be my friend?"
- "Wanna come to my party?"

"Use your walking feet in the halls," reminds Mr. Cooper as a group of students heads off to the library with their books. Initially, all is well as the children walk in lockstep with each other. However, with his longer leg stride, Larson moves slightly ahead of the rest. This prompts the other students to walk a little faster. Hearing the faster click-clack of shoes behind him, Larson speeds up to match the group's rhythm.

Like a roller coaster gains speed heading down a steep turn, so do the students as they pick up momentum. Fast walking becomes faster walking, which then turns into speed walking. And before long, the whole group of kids is racing down the school corridor as fast as their legs can.

This is a perfect example of how children's need to belong often drives inappropriate behaviors. Their need to connect with their friends makes them start running and chasing. They might know what they are supposed to do, but doing the right thing is influenced by development.

> ***Initially, children's emotional need to belong is stronger than their cognitive voice of reason.***

Children develop a sense of right and wrong at an early age. However, the frontal lobes that control this sense are underdeveloped in young brains. This helps explain why getting kids to stop running in the halls can be difficult. Initially, children's emotional need to belong is stronger than their cognitive voice of reason. This is also the reason that peer pressure, at any age, is such a powerful force. It goes back to our need to gain acceptance and belonging.

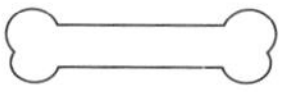

One of the best ways to foster a sense of belonging is to provide children with opportunities to interact with diverse groups of kids in various settings. When children see other children who look and act similarly to the way they do, they naturally feel a sense of belonging. When exposed to others who look and act differently, they become more comfortable and tolerant of differences.

I recall being at recess when two little girls ran up to me and smiled. "This is my friend," one said. "We're school friends," the other little girl added. "School friends?" I inquired. "Yes. We're school friends," the first girl said and nodded. "We also have gymnastic friends, church friends, and some home friends that go to other schools. But we're just school friends!" the second girl exclaimed as they ran off again to play.

This quick discussion with the girls made me smile, knowing they had a large variety of friends. And the stronger the variety, the better the chance for them to find ways to connect and belong.

Teachers should avoid behavioral practices that inadvertently make students feel singled out in negative ways for being different:

- Behavior Clip Systems
- Names on the Board
- Continued Public Redirection

Though well-intentioned, these strategies can isolate children and create a "good kids/bad kids" mindset that works against our efforts to help children feel connected with others.

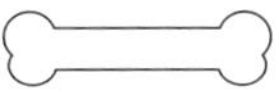

Another way to foster belonging in children is to use language that identifies commonalities in a variety of ways:

<u>Physical Appearance</u>

- "Look, Vera! Maddi has a red coat just like you."
- "You both got haircuts!"

- "We have three friends in this class who have blue eyes. I wonder who they are?"

Likes and Dislikes

- "Aisha and Louis both chose the color red."
- "Sunny, Maurice likes pickles too!"
- "That's okay, Jayden. Idris doesn't want to go either.

Challenges

- "It's okay. Several friends are still learning how to tie their shoes."
- "Just like you need glasses to see, Devon needs braces to help him walk."
- "You're not the only one. We have two other students who get help from Mr. Syd."

By overtly pointing out these similarities, we increase the chance kids will start noticing them independently. And by doing so, these connections naturally help kids develop empathy and understanding for others.

There are a variety of other ways teachers can foster community and belonging in the classroom setting:

- Class Celebrations
- "All About Me" Boards
- Reading Buddies
- Class Performances
- Family-Style Lunches
- Chants
- Routines
- Class Jobs
- Centers
- Group Projects

LESSON LEARNED

Behaviors are swayed by our need for connection.

Belonging is critical to our well-being, so a healthy goal for adults is to connect children with their "tribes." These are other individuals who help kids feel recognized, appreciated, loved, and accepted. The more we can foster this need for belonging to be met when kids are young, the stronger the support system they will have as they age.

CHAPTER SEVEN

ATTENTION

It's a familiar story among dog owners. I had just sat down one morning to begin working on my computer when I felt a furry nudge on my leg. As I could have predicted, I saw LaRoux staring at me with her favorite squirrel tug toy dangling from her mouth when I looked down.

"You know I want to play with you," I told her. "But I can't right now. Let me get a few things taken care of first." Sadly, this did not appease her. Nudge, nudge. "Later, LaRoux," I reiterated. Though I am confident this was not the response she was looking for, she finally sulked off, squirrel in mouth, head hanging low.

Fast-forward fifteen minutes, when I realized I hadn't seen LaRoux in a while. I also became aware of how eerily quiet it was. *[Atypical silence readily alarms parents of young ones, whether two legs or four.]* "Where's our sweet pup?" I called out. Immediately upon hearing my voice, LaRoux popped up from across the room, jumped over the couch, and came crashing into my legs, carrying my wife's chewed-up shoe in her mouth.

Though I wanted to blame her for this mishap, I couldn't. Truth be known, the only reason LaRoux went after that shoe was because I wasn't playing with her. This incident could have been avoided if I had given her a few minutes of my time that morning.

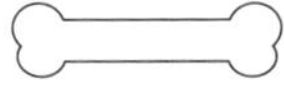

Our need for attention is closely related to our need for belonging. Both help us meet our overarching need to be seen and heard by others. This is critical for children because the younger they are, the more their survival depends on it.

The young brain communicates needs through behaviors.

The young brain communicates needs through behaviors. When babies are tired or hungry, they cry. And when these behaviors are attended to, the needs are met. This interdependence between infants needing attention and adults providing it lays the foundation for healthy development.

As children get older, they become more self-sufficient. However, they still need our attention because, on a psychological level, attention lets them know they are important and valued. This feeling contributes to their healthy self-esteem.

One of the challenges of giving attention is time, which is in very short supply for most people. Think about your typical day. How much time do you spend giving your undivided attention to others? The key word in that sentence is *undivided*. We all interact with others, but often we do so while trying to accomplish other things, toggling our attention back and forth between people and tasks.

Grown-ups tend to be more understanding of partial attention because we can empathize with other adults, their needs, and their time constraints. Children, however, don't have this capacity because of their limited life experience, combined with their natural inclination to focus on self-needs.

Children know on an emotional level how it feels not to have someone's full attention. My son pointed this out to me when he was a young teen. "You never listen to me," he argued. "Yes, I do," I said. "No, you don't," he continued. "When I tell you something, you're too busy thinking about what you will say next. You're not really listening; you're just waiting for me to finish talking." Though I wanted to respond, I couldn't. Sadly, he was right.

Because we have a finite amount of time each day, our brains must prioritize how we spend it. Those things in our lives that are most important get our attention. And when you think about it that way, it's easy to understand why children want and need our attention.

A greeting shared in the South African culture highlights this need. In the first part, a person approaches another and says, "Sikhona," which means, "I am here to be seen." The response they get from others is "Sawubona," which means "I see you."

I am sure kids are telling us "Sikhona" through their behaviors. I also know there are specific things we can do to respond in a way that helps them feel both seen and acknowledged. We just need to be more purposeful in doing so.

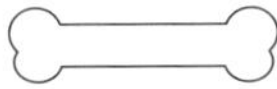

When providing more attention to kids, the starting place for adults is practicing mindfulness. It's easy to get caught up in the daily rush and overwhelmed with our never-ending to-do list, but this state is not conducive to focusing our attention. Slowing down, clearing our minds, and being consciously aware of what's happening in the present is the best way to set the stage for paying attention.

When adults practice mindfulness, kids reap the benefits:

- We help children get their need for our attention met.
- We teach children how to slow down and self-regulate their behaviors.
- We teach children how to be present and pay better attention.
- When modeled consistently, we help children develop habits of mindfulness.

When my oldest son was in second grade, I recall him getting very frustrated with me and his three younger brothers. He needed help with something, but my time and attention were being split among our four children. "Do you ever wonder what being the only son in our house would be like?" I asked him. He just looked at me, blinked, and smiled. "I know you love your brothers, but sometimes do you just need one-on-one dad time?"

We had a good talk. I told him that any time he needed "just dad time," to let me know. And when he did, within the same day, we would do something—just the two of us. I had that same talk with all four of my sons. And when one of the boys took me up on the offer, the two of us would go to the grocery store, walk to the mailbox, or eat a snack. And for a brief moment, that child got my undivided attention.

What I remember about those small, individual interactions with my sons was not the number of times we had them or the amount of time I spent with them. What seemed important was the quality of our time together. It was free of distractions. This meant the other boys weren't right there, and interruptions were limited.

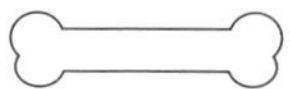

The best strategy for meeting the need for attention is simply providing it. Though time and tasks are competing for most adults' attention, we need to remember that there is no substitute for genuine, one-on-one positive attention for children.

The best strategy for meeting the need for attention is simply providing it.

This is challenging for teachers since they usually deal with large class sizes. However, young children's attention spans are small, so frequency is more important than duration. This means we don't need to carve out long periods to connect with individual kids. Talking with a child for two minutes during a transition each day can profoundly impact meeting their need for attention.

There is one cautionary tale to remember when it comes to giving attention*: The squeaky wheel gets the grease.* Often in classrooms, adults get so ingrained in their daily routines that we only attend to children's behaviors when they become disruptive. This usually translates to one or two children getting all the attention—for negative behaviors. This pattern of attention can create several problems:

- It can have a negative impact on a child's self-esteem.
- Adult-child relationships can be damaged.
- Some children receive negative attention from their peers and are labeled "the bad kids."
- Adults become more prone to notice negative behaviors.
- Some children get in the habit of getting their need for attention met in negative ways.

Positive attention is what we want. However, this doesn't mean we spend all our time "catching kids being good." Continual praise can create problems, just as continual criticism can. The key is balance. When recognition is given that is genuine, intermittent, and individualized, it can go a long way in strengthening positive behaviors and healthy relationships. But it is also good to remember that when adults spend quality time with children, that, in itself, is meeting the need for attention in a healthy way.

For young children, meeting the need for attention starts with watching, listening, and responding. When we attend to a crying child, we teach them we care. When we respond by mirroring a happy smile, we teach them their feelings matter. Every action from a child that turns into an interaction between adult and child feeds the attention need.

Concentrating with distractions is hard, especially in our world of advanced technology. A lot of stimuli are competing for our eyes and ears. Video games, Instagram, movies, Twitter, and advertisements—all want to grab and keep our attention. This can make an adult's job difficult because, let's face it, if a child is choosing between time with us or time playing a high-octane video game, the outcome will not be in our favor.

This is one of many reasons why it is vital for parents to limit technology use with their children—and to model limited use ourselves. The younger a child is, the less time they should be interacting with screens. Kids need face-to-face interaction time with others, and screen time can sabotage undivided attention.

LESSON LEARNED

Attention is power.

Some children get in the habit of meeting their need for attention in negative ways. We all need to be both seen and heard. When we intentionally pay attention to children, we help meet these needs and strengthen positive relationships in the process.

CHAPTER EIGHT

PHYSICAL ACTIVITY

Puppy energy—I'm convinced we could light up the entire West Coast with just a tiny bit. LaRoux, like most young pups, had a great deal of it, and it often came out in bursts. "The zoomies," as we called them, would be on full display, usually right after she ate. A little fuel would hit her stomach, and that was all it took. Off she went—up on one side of the couch, down the other, around the coffee table, and back up again. This pattern repeated until she wore herself down.

In another version of the zoomies, LaRoux would grab a toy from her basket and run around the living room playing catch with herself, slinging the toy hither and yon. One would think the toy was real from how she interacted with it. She needed no help from us to stay entertained; she just needed a wide-open space to expel some energy. Trying to stop, slow down, or simply contain her behavior was pointless.

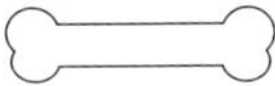

If one need in children presents itself directly, it's the need for physical activity. Want proof? Check out a nearby grocery store, classroom, church service, or doctor's office. Evidence of children's compulsion to move is all around us. And unfortunately, this need usually spills out in ways classified as misbehavior.

This isn't just an issue with children, of course. We all require movement. However, adults learn to regulate. Being self-aware and mindful of social graces, adults create accommodations that allow our needs to be met. When confined in meetings, we shake our legs under tables, check our phones, doodle on papers, and take bathroom breaks.

Adults also have a significant advantage because we have more-developed brains than children. This means we can better suppress our need for movement when it arises.

Younger developing brains are more prone to act on impulses, so they have a more challenging time doing this.

Societal trends do not help this issue. At odds with the need for physical activity is research indicating that kids are engaged in more sedentary activities than kids of yesteryear. This equates to children not having natural outlets that help them fill the need for movement.

One clear example of this is the nature of play and how it has changed so dramatically over the last fifty years. "Where are the kids?" adults used to ask. "They went outside to play," was the answer. Riding bikes, climbing trees, and playing hide-and-seek or chase were all typical activities.

Now, play looks different. Children mostly play indoors in more confined spaces and in less physical ways. This is due to various factors, including safety issues, supervision, and increased technology use. For the most part, outdoor physical play seems to have been replaced by indoor electronic play.

"My kids are always on their screens!" one mother told me. "I can't get them off of them. I can't tell you the number of times I've reached down to pick up my tablet to read a book or searched in my purse for my phone to check my messages and discovered my kids were on my devices. It's crazy!"

It's hard to miss the irony here. Yes, children spend a great deal of time in front of screens, but then again, so are their role models. I'm not pointing fingers at others. I'm just as guilty of excessive technology use. But we must acknowledge that as adults, we contribute to this problem when we model the behaviors we are trying to reshape in our children.

Another factor that seems to be contributing to kids having fewer physical outlets is less recess time in the school setting. In an attempt to meet high academic standards and maximize instruction time, recesses are getting shortened or cut altogether. Recess is also taken away from many students as punishment for their misbehavior. (In my experience, the children who regularly lose recess are often the very ones who need that outlet the most.)

...the children who regularly lose recess are often the very ones who need that outlet the most.

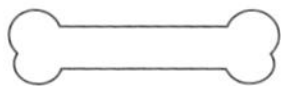

Plasticity refers to the brain's ability to adapt and change with experiences, and there is a clear connection between this concept and age. The younger the brain, the greater the brain plasticity. This equates to more remarkable outcomes for active children in several developmental areas.

Kids engaged in physical activity, especially when integrated into learning activities:

Cognitively

- Are better able to pay and sustain attention to tasks
- Have a quicker reaction time
- Make stronger cognitive connections

Emotionally/Psychologically

- Have higher levels of self-esteem
- Experience a more positive affect
- Have reduced risk of depression

Physically

- Have stronger bones, better heart health, coordination, balance, and flexibility
- Are at less risk for becoming overweight
- Sleep better at night

This makes a great deal of sense. Activity increases blood flow and oxygen in the brain, triggers the release of feel-good chemicals, relieves stress, and increases energy levels. All these factors contribute to overall healthy development in children. Additionally, the more we can keep kids active when they are young, the better chance these behaviors will become lifelong habits that will continue to benefit them as they age.

Activity increases blood flow and oxygen in the brain, triggers the release of feel-good chemicals, relieves stress, and increases energy levels.

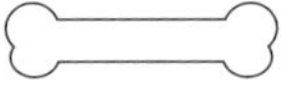

Parents are in the best position to work with their children on having healthy habits that involve physical activity because they are the ones who establish their initial routines. And having a routine is the first step. When kids have a set schedule of waking each morning, their natural body clock will alert them it is time to get out of bed and start moving.

Throughout the day, the goal is for kids to have good regular outlets for staying active while balancing this need with periods of calm and quiet. What should be avoided are extended periods of sustained sedentary behaviors. This is when poor habits begin to develop.

Speaking of sustained sedentary behaviors, it's vital for parents to limit their children's technology use. Though this was noted in the last chapter, it is worth repeating because of the multiple benefits of this one strategy.

When children get used to a lot of time in front of screens, they form the habit of physical passivity. Screens also tend to have a high novelty factor, drawing young eyes in and making it difficult for them to pull away. Most people have had the experience of picking up their phone to check one thing, only to find themselves still on the device sometime later.

Limiting screen time is much easier to do when children are younger before strong viewing habits are established. Once that happens, behaviors are much harder to change. Any parent of a teenager can attest to this.

There are many good practices for limiting children's screen time:

- Don't put televisions in children's bedrooms. Since kids spend a good deal of time there, it encourages high use, especially around bedtime.
- Have a "no electronics before bed" expectation. Screen time stimulates the brain and disrupts melatonin production.
- Electronic devices should remain with parents, not where kids can pick them up and use them at leisure.
- Keep electronics turned off while eating together at the dinner table. This is a beneficial social skill, and the practice encourages family discussion.

- Set time limits for electronics use. Having children choose one cartoon to watch or play one video game keeps them from getting deeply absorbed in the activity, which can lead to prolonged periods of sitting. Additionally, the longer they are engaged in screens, the harder for them to disengage.
- Lastly, the best way for children to have screen time is with adults. Watch shows and play games together. This allows for good monitoring of content and healthy bonding time.

Getting children involved in sports is another effective way to encourage physical activity. Doing so also teaches children skills in other developmental areas:

- Social - Playing Well with Others
- Emotional—Accepting Disappointment
- Behavioral—Accepting Feedback from Non-Parent Adults
- Ethical—Making Good Choices

Teachers and parents can integrate movement into learning through interactive songs, chants, and games. They can also take children on learning walks and field trips, remembering that an active body stimulates a growing brain.

Transitions are also a great time for teachers to incorporate fun movement into learning. Kids can hop to their spots like kangaroos, crawl to their spots like bugs, tiptoe to their spots like quiet mice, or dance to their spots when upbeat music starts. The main idea is to increase movement opportunities throughout the day in fun ways.

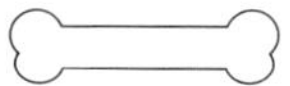

LaRoux, and her brother, Odin, are very lucky we have a dog park near our home. It's their favorite spot to run free and spend time with neighborhood friends. When I get the dogs' leashes, their tails begin to wag in excitement. They love going to the dog park. However, leaving it is another story.

Actually, LaRoux doesn't mind when it's time to leave the park. She just wants to be with her people. So, wherever we go, she usually follows. Odin, however, would probably prefer to live at the dog park if given the opportunity. It's a struggle to get him to leave. Usually, Odin passes by a good citizen who grabs his collar while I put his leash back on.

I say ***usually*** because, on a few Saturdays, Odin has self-selected to walk up to the gate and turn to look at me as if to say, *"I'm ready now. Can we go?"* Of course, this happens on Saturdays when I have more time to devote to the trip, coupled with the times Odin has run nonstop around the park.

The obvious learning point for this dog owner? When my pup's need for physical activity is met, he no longer has to "misbehave" and run away to get the need met on his own. The same tends to be true with the children in our homes and classrooms.

LESSON LEARNED

Bodies need to move.

It's natural for kids of all ages to want and need to move. And since physical activity helps young brains function better, the more we encourage kids to engage in it, the better off they will be.

CHAPTER NINE

CONTROL

Did I mention LaRoux occasionally had an aggressive streak? It rarely came out, but it was intense when it did. We noticed it during one of her advanced training classes. Immediately upon entering the area with the other pups, LaRoux's hackles would rise. Each time this happened, I took her out of the class to have a "talk," but the behavior always reemerged when we returned. And since this happened week after week, by the end of the sessions, LaRoux had her time-out spot outside the classroom door because it was as close to the other dogs as she could be without incident.

We had a hard time understanding why she had difficulty in this class since she had done so well in the others. She also displayed zero aggression with other animals at the dog park. The concerns seemed to be isolated to this one environment. One night, while listening to a news feature on the drive home, I realized the source of the problem.

The first thing I heard when I turned on the radio caught my attention. "The most frightening thing to a nervous patient entering surgery is to have a nervous doctor." The nurse being interviewed continued, "It's a matter of control. When we don't feel in control of a situation, we get anxious and want to feel assured that all will be well. A nervous doctor doesn't exactly do that."

As I listened to the nurse talk, I thought about LaRoux's problem with aggression in the advanced class and a previous lesson learned through puppy training. *That's it,* I thought to myself. *Emotions feed emotions.* LaRoux was feeding off the nervous energy of the other dogs in the class—most of whom were small and fairly anxious.

But there was more to it than that. I believe her anxiety was heightened because she was on a leash, and being controlled, rather than having control and being able to defend herself if needed. This triggered her reaction of aggression and explained why she didn't have problems at the dog park—where she wasn't on a leash or in a confined space. In that class, LaRoux needed to feel a sense of control.

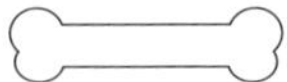

Accepting a position in an early childhood center for the last seventeen years of my career was one of the best decisions I'd ever made. Having worked with different ages in different settings before that, I wanted to look at behavior through the lens of the young child. And in doing so, I quickly discovered how right Robert Fulghum was in his award-winning book *All I Need to Know I Learned in Kindergarten.* Though I had many "aha" moments while working there, I credit much of my growth in dealing with challenging behaviors to a handful of children. Damien was one of those children.

I met Damien a few hours into the first day of school as I walked around the building checking on teachers and students. "I might have a friend for you," Ms. Hebert said. I looked in the room and saw a boy standing in the middle of the carpet around a classroom full of sitting students. "He was already sitting on the carpet when I asked the other kids to do the same. As soon as I said 'sit,' he stood up," she continued. "Whatever direction I give, he does the opposite—then he looks at me and smiles."

I recognized this pattern of behavior. "So, in a nutshell, he won't follow your directions, and he thinks it's funny. Is that what we are dealing with?" I asked her. Ms. Hebert just looked at me and smiled.

Over the following month, the same behaviors continued. Ms. Hebert and I provided firm boundaries and consequences but with little success. I knew I was missing something, and it wasn't until I met with Damien's mother that I started to understand his behaviors differently.

"Does he smile when you correct him?" she asked me. "Actually, yes. He does," I told her. "He does that when he's in trouble," she continued. "He also smiles when I turn out his bedroom light at night just before he runs out of his room. He smiles when he gets nervous or scared."

As I sat and listened to his mom tell me about the many problems the family had faced in Damien's five short years in this world, I better understood his oppositional behaviors. They were his way of taking control. This didn't excuse the behaviors, but it did help me adjust my perspective and the strategies we used to provide support.

Following this discussion with Damien's mother, the teacher and I found ways to give Damien more choices. We looked for ways to provide him with control that worked for him and Ms. Hebert. And as we did so, his oppositional behaviors slowly began to subside.

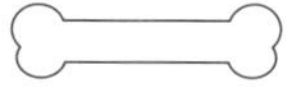

Control helps us feel safe.

Control helps us feel safe. We feel helpless and vulnerable when we don't have it. This triggers the brain to go into fight-or-flight mode, which can result in kids lashing out or shutting down. Fortunately, if we look beyond surface behaviors and understand children's need for control, we can provide it in positive ways—and avert negative behaviors in the process.

As we've discussed, when children are very young, they are dependent on others for survival. And this connection with others helps them meet their need for a sense of belonging. However, as they get older, the hope is for them to become more self-sufficient and less reliant on others to get their needs met. This sense of independence is highlighted in *The Circle of Courage.*

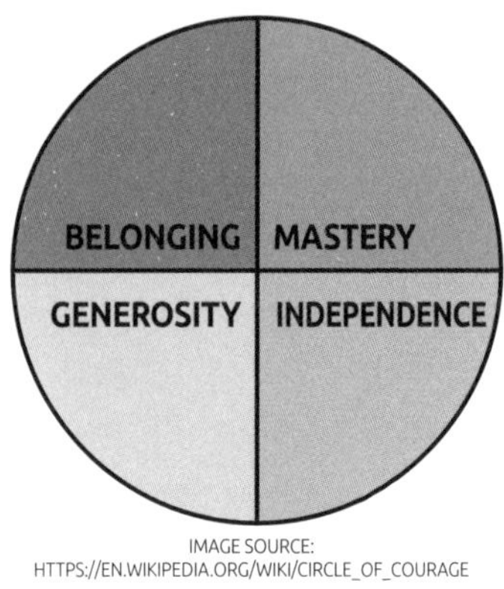

IMAGE SOURCE: HTTPS://EN.WIKIPEDIA.ORG/WIKI/CIRCLE_OF_COURAGE

Our need for independence is directly connected to our need for control. We want to feel as though we can make choices that make a difference and that we have influence over our life. We also want to know that when we face challenges, we have the power to effect change.

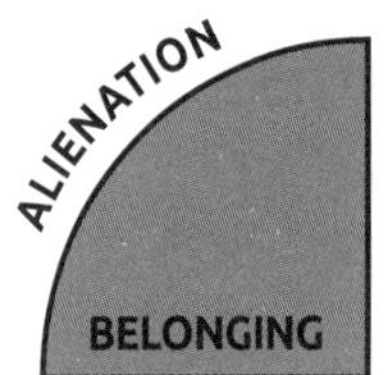

Children who aren't given a sense of independence can experience a loss of control. This can lead to a feeling of helplessness or dependence, neither of which leads to positive outcomes. It can also lead to power struggles between children and adults, with children trying to exert their independence when not afforded appropriate opportunities to do so.

One of the most important strategies for helping children feel in control is to give them control through choices. Of course, it is essential that when providing choices, the

> ***One of the most important strategies for helping children feel in control is to give them control through choices.***

options need to be two acceptable ones. If a child doesn't have a choice, a directive should be given.

When providing choices, the options should be minimal, as providing too many can be overwhelming. Limited choices are the best way to give children a degree of control without inadvertently raising anxiety—which is what can happen with open-ended choices. The key is involving the child in the decision-making process.

- "Do you want to sit in this chair or at the table?"
- "Would you rather have milk or water?"
- "Red or green?"

The goal should be to provide choices proactively so children have regular opportunities to feel in control. This is a strategic way to prevent oppositional behaviors. The more kids have control over more minor issues, the less likely they may be to try taking control when upset and not wanting to follow directions.

When children exert control by not following directions, adults must remember the adage that it takes two to argue. Rather than engaging in a *"No, I'm not!" "Yes, you are!"* discussion when children don't follow directions, respond with empathy in a way that avoids a debate. Doing so prevents you from power struggles that often reinforce children's negative behaviors. For example:

Child: *"I'm not doing that!"*
Adult: *"You're mad. I get mad too sometimes."* **or**
"It's okay to be angry." **or**
"I understand. You're upset."

This approach keeps the focus on the feelings rather than the actual words. This is important because often, when children are upset, they say things they don't mean. Their comments come out impulsively as expressions of their emotions:

- "I hate you!"
- "You're stupid."
- "I'm going to hit you."

In these instances, rather than responding to the words, respond to the feelings behind the words: *"You're upset. I understand."* Responding to the words only validates them. Another option is to not respond at all. Sometimes, the small act of letting children have the last word gives them the small degree of control needed to de-escalate a situation. If needed, you can always address the specific words at a later time when the child is calm.

I'm reminded of a time many years ago when my wife and I had difficulty getting one of our sons out of bed for church on Sundays. After much prompting and prodding one morning, he begrudgingly got up and ran to the car in his pajamas. After my wife told him our expectation that he needed to put on clothes for church, he stormed back into his room, flinging open drawers and pulling out clothes. When he returned, he wore a short-sleeved dress shirt, shorts, and cowboy boots, all put on over his long-sleeved pajamas. Just as I was about to intervene and have him go back to his room, my wife looked at him and calmly said, "Thank you. Let's get in the car." My wise wife remembered what I had forgotten. We needed to give him control over the less important things so he didn't take control in ways that could be more concerning as he got older.

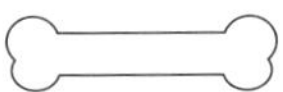

I feel somewhat hypocritical writing this chapter. Out of all behavioral needs, control is the one I have the most difficult time relinquishing, which is probably why one of my sons has the same issue. Father and son both needed control—definitely not the best combination.

Fortunately, a young boy named Damien and, years later, a puppy named LaRoux, were dropped into my life. And through them, I learned a valuable lesson about the developing brain and its need for control. When my son was behaving in challenging ways, to some degree, that was his way of telling me he needed more control than I was giving him. I just needed to do a better job of listening and responding accordingly.

LESSON LEARNED

Loss of control feeds oppositional behaviors.

Brains are survival-oriented and need a sense of control to feel safe. Challenging behaviors often come from children's attempts to meet this need. We can help children feel in control by regularly giving them choices and involving them in decision-making.

CHAPTER TEN

INSTRUCTION

One of the dangers of having an intelligent dog is that you assume they are good at everything. This is problematic because having this perspective lets you get used to them picking up concepts quickly, and frustration sets in when they don't.

As noted, LaRoux did very well in the first few weeks of puppy training. However, she hit a wall when it came time to bow. The desired behavior was to arch the front of her body to the ground while keeping the back end in a standing position.

For some reason, LaRoux could not seem to grasp this skill. With her body so low to the ground, she put her head down or dropped her whole body completely. After working with

her on this skill for a while with little success, the trainer had to step in and coach both of us.

"This skill can be hard for small dogs," she said. "But there are some things that we can do to help LaRoux be successful." The trainer broke down the skill into a few smaller steps, modeled what they looked like, and then had me try again.

As I worked with LaRoux on this skill over the next few weeks, I noticed a disturbing pattern in my thought process. As I saw other dogs easily bow with one gesture from their trainer, I found myself getting frustrated that LaRoux needed more support. *She doesn't need all these steps,* I thought.

The reality, however, was that she *did* need them. Whenever I took the time to break down and teach all the steps in the process, LaRoux was successful. But when I tried to shortcut the process, bowing didn't happen. LaRoux needed more intensive teaching from me, and it needed to be differentiated.

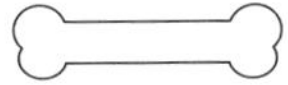

Kids need instruction. It's how they learn. This is true not only with academic skills but also in how children learn behavioral skills. However, when it comes to teaching children how to behave, the teaching and learning process is a bit more complicated. Given the world we live in and the society in which our kids are being raised, they are learning behaviors from a variety of sources.

Children learn directly and indirectly; unfortunately, the latter often works against our efforts to instill positive and polite behaviors. Because of their need to belong, children look to others for connection. And in doing so, they quickly soak up modeled behaviors like sponges.

Spend one hour looking at the world through the eyes of a young brain, and it becomes easy to understand why we see more challenging behaviors in children. I often do this—in airports, grocery stores, and restaurants; while watching movies, reality TV, and news programs—and wonder, *What lessons are we teaching kids through the behaviors being modeled?*

- We tell children not to throw fits…yet they hear adults yell and curse.
- We tell children to be kind…yet they hear sarcasm that puts down others.
- We tell children to be patient and considerate…yet they hear horn honking and see tailgating and emphatic gestures from drivers.
- We tell children to respect differing opinions…yet they hear adults regularly put down others with whom they disagree.

Additional behavioral lessons can be found in movies and television programs:

- We tell children to use their words to solve problems…yet they see physical violence as the primary way to do so.

- We tell children that reckless driving and drugs are dangerous…yet both are glamorized.

We often teach children one set of behaviors through our words and another through our actions. So, while we work to teach children positive behaviors, their still-developing brains have to sort out contradicting messages and unlearn poor behaviors that have been internalized on an unconscious level.

We often teach children one set of behaviors through our words and another through our actions.

"I can't believe how my grandson acts," a lady once told me. "I would have never done the things he does when I was young." She continued, "We were much better behaved—if I had misbehaved back then the way my grandson does now, my parents would have let me have it!"

I have heard this comment from countless adults, and because of my age, I understand their reality. The older we are, the more there is a disconnect between our behaviors as a child and the behaviors we see now. I behaved well when I was young because positive behaviors were the standard—for adults and kids.

This is an important point. Most adults who grew up in my generation and I learned how to behave through modeling. We were taught through example. We didn't need tons of explicit behavior training because we learned by assimilating to the standard.

This is why intentionally teaching appropriate behavior to kids may not come naturally to adults. Because our inclination is to look through the lens of what we know, it's hard for many adults, especially older ones, to understand why children don't just pick up appropriate behaviors as we did. It's an issue of separate realities.

Teaching appropriate behaviors to children is also hindered by adults' competing responsibilities. With most parents working and teachers focused on meeting academic goals, there's little time for behavioral instruction. This is why it is essential for adults to work together to meet this need.

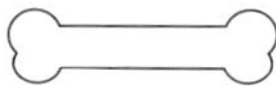

When teaching behavioral expectations to children, we should use very specific language and do so consistently:

- "We raise our hands to get attention."
- "We pay attention with our eyes and our ears."
- "We use our walking feet in the halls."
- "We use our words to tell people how we feel."

Unfortunately, adults don't always use clear, objective, and specific language when describing behaviors. Instead, behaviors are often referred to using subjective, vague, and judgmental words and phrases:

- "Stop doing that."
- "She doesn't care."
- "Behave."
- "He thinks it's funny when I correct him."
- "Be respectful."

How these behaviors are described doesn't help meet kids' need for clarity. And if used repeatedly, they can damage our relationships with children and have a negative impact on their self-esteem. A better approach is to use specific language around behavioral skill strengths and concerns:

- "Hale is doing a good job with the skill of respecting personal space."
- "One of Randall's behavioral skill strengths is his ability to be a good friend."
- "Karlinda's working on the skill of accepting feedback appropriately."
- "Class, today you did a great job following directions at lunch."
- "Remember, Lucas, follow mama's directions right away."

Simply by labeling behaviors in specific skill terms, we reinforce the notion of the need for instruction. This also moves us away from describing behaviors in even more general and subjective terms of being "good" and "bad."

As we touched on in Chapter 1, parents and teachers often try to communicate behavioral expectations when children are in a heightened emotional state and are already upset. This can lead to power struggles. The best time to voice expectations is at a neutral time when children and adults are both calm. This approach yields the best results, ensuring that children are more receptive to our teaching efforts than when they are upset.

One of the best ways to teach children positive behaviors is by playing games with them.

One of the best ways to teach children positive behaviors is by playing games with them. Games naturally instill behavioral skills while helping children meet their need for positive emotional states of joy. Outdoor games have the bonus of helping to meet kids' need for physical activity. For example:

Game	Primary Lesson
Simon Says	Following Directions
Mother, May I?	Using Good Manners
I Spy	Paying Attention
Red Rover	Respecting Personal Space
Duck, Duck, Goose	Being Considerate
Hide and Seek	Being Quiet and Listening

In addition to the benefits noted above, games allow children to accept disappointment appropriately when they don't win and be gracious when they do. Both of these lessons are critical ones for children to learn.

Playing games with children is also a natural way to assess their skill strengths and areas of concern. Because kids have different gifts and challenges, knowing individual differences allows us to differentiate our instruction. Just as we provide children with academic modifications and accommodations, so should we provide them with behavioral ones. In doing so, we help each child to be successful. Here are some examples:

Skill Challenge	Modification
Managing Feelings Appropriately	Let the child hug a stuffed animal when scared or upset.
Respecting Personal Space by Keeping Hands to Self	Give the child a special job of holding something, which keeps hands occupied.
Paying Attention	Provide a special spot on the carpet for the child to sit, which is directly in front of the teacher.
Following Directions and Staying with the Class	Have the child hold the hand of an adult when walking down the hall.

LESSON LEARNED

Desired behaviors must be taught, not just expected.

Just as children need to be taught their letters, numbers, and other academic skills, so too do they need behavioral instruction. And children are far more receptive than adults to learning behavioral skills while their brains are still young and malleable. This task gets much more challenging as brains age and behavioral habits become ingrained.

CHAPTER ELEVEN

PRACTICE

One of the more important lessons I learned from LaRoux happened when she was in her first puppy class. Since she was so young, I focused on meeting her basic needs. However, looking back now, I realize that in trying to meet one need, I was depriving her of getting a second and equally important need met.

The pups at the St. Romain house had a consistent morning routine. After returning home from the gym, the dogs would enthusiastically greet me at the door. Though I am sure they were excited by my presence, seeing me meant they knew what would happen next: breakfast. And after breakfast was puppy practice time—which the dogs also loved.

Once LaRoux finished eating, she ran to my feet, sat nicely, and stared. And she continued to stare until I gave some acknowledgment of her presence. This was her not-so-subtle hint that she was ready to practice all the tricks she had learned that week in puppy class.

We had a predictable pattern in our practice sessions. First, I sat on the kitchen floor by her kennel with her toys, treats, and a clicker that served as an auditory cue for making good choices. Next, I'd run through all the skills she learned. And lastly, we would backtrack and practice the more difficult ones. *Having been a teacher for so long, I knew how to teach.*

She did great in class, as well as in our kitchen practice sessions. But those were the only times and places LaRoux tended to demonstrate the skills consistently. At other times—when we were at the park, going for a walk, or when company came over—we had a fifty-fifty shot of LaRoux following directions.

I thought the problem was that LaRoux just needed more practice. However, something the instructor said in class made me realize it was more than that. "Remember," she said, "our long-term goal is for our dogs to be successful outside our training sessions." That's when it hit me—practice can't just be isolated to one place and one time.

In trying to meet LaRoux's need for a routine, I was depriving her of her need to practice in a variety of settings. The routine I established set the expectation that she only needed to follow directions in two places (the kitchen and pet store) at two times (after breakfast and in class) with familiar motivators in place (treats and clicker). LaRoux needed real-life practice in a variety of settings if I wanted her to internalize the skills for continual use.

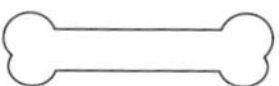

> ***...when we practice something, we get better at it.***

The need for practice is a straightforward one. Simply put, when we practice something, we get better at it. Conversely, if we don't practice, our skills don't improve. As you might have guessed, this has implications when it comes to children's behavior.

For kids to get better at behaving well, they need practice. And they need practice in the environment and ways they will most likely use it. When it comes to behavior, this means through interactions with others.

As previously discussed in several chapters, this is where technology is working against our efforts. Time in front of a screen takes away from time kids can spend interacting with their peers. Accordingly, they miss out on opportunities to learn critical social skills:

- How to have a conversation with others
- How to use their words to solve problems
- How to be kind to others
- How to play nicely
- How to stand up for themselves

The pandemic magnified this lack of practice time when we were isolated and had much less face-to-face interaction. Kids interacted somewhat virtually, but virtual interactions look very different from real ones—especially with adults always around.

Technology also changes the way children learn to interact with others. We see this with teenagers saying things about their peers on social media they would never say to their peers' faces. However, technology takes away the immediate consequence kids would otherwise receive.

Another factor is that some children interact more with adults than their peers. This creates different challenges. On many occasions, teachers have approached me with some version of this story:

"Celia is a new student in my room. She's super bright and very articulate. In some ways, she's like an adult trapped in a little girl's body. The reason I'm coming to you is that Celia has a difficult time getting along with other children. The kids in my class try to include her, but she doesn't like sharing and often says hurtful things. When the students are in centers, Celia will often come to tell me that the other kids are taking all the toys. And when we are at recess, she spends her play time talking to me and our assistant teacher. We encourage her to play with the other children, but she doesn't want to."

In talking with Celia's mother, I learned a lot. She was a single mom, and Celia was her only child. After school, Celia was picked up by her grandparents and stayed with them until her mom got off work. Due to safety issues, mom said she didn't feel comfortable letting Celia play with the other children in the apartment complex. This was Celia's first school experience.

This is a great example of the impact of lack of practice. Celia was very comfortable talking with adults because they were the ones with whom she had all the practice. This also explained why she was so articulate. Regarding peer social interaction, however, she was starting from the beginning.

The teacher agreed with my assessment but wasn't sure how to help Celia. "How do you help the other students when they have skill deficits?" I asked. "I work on teaching them ways to adjust and improve in those areas," she answered. I followed up, "If Celia has behavioral skill deficits, she needs time to be taught appropriate behaviors and time to practice." Together, the teacher and I mapped out a plan:

1. Identify the specific social skills Celia needed. (i.e., Being a Good Friend, Using Kind Words)
2. Teach her the skills.
3. Provide accommodations to help her experience success (partnering with one kind peer; prompting).
4. Give her extensive practice time, allowing natural and logical consequences to help her learn.
5. Be patient. We knew it would take time for her to learn and, more importantly, practice the skills before they became internalized.

In this situation, the most significant change that occurred was one of perspective. Once the teacher realized the problem was due to a skill deficit, she focused less on rewarding and punishing Celia's behaviors and more on the tasks of teaching and practicing.

Just because we look at behavior through a lens of practice does not mean kids should not receive consequences for poor choices. However, too often, I believe adults focus on *punishing*

poor behaviors rather than *practicing* appropriate ones. The former is more reactive, the latter more proactive. Punishment is designed *to stop* poor behaviors, while practice focuses on *instilling* good ones.

As noted in the last chapter, playing games is a great way to learn if we want kids to develop good social skills with others. Playing games also allows kids to practice the skills they've learned continuously. This helps them strengthen and refine their skills in a natural and developmentally appropriate setting.

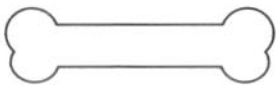

I've never been a fan of the adage, "Practice makes perfect." For one reason, *perfect* is an elusive end goal—one that is neither achievable nor that I find helpful. I want children to focus on the *process* of improvement rather than the *product* of perfection.

My modification? "Practice makes *progress*." I love to use this phrase to encourage kids to keep trying. It goes along with, "The more we practice, the better we get." However, when I'm trying to help adults understand why the need to practice appropriate behaviors is so important, I teach them a different phrase: "Practice makes permanent."

I don't want our end goal to be for children to behave at isolated times. If I did, I would advocate for models of rewarding and punishing. I would do this knowing that in the absence of a reward or punishment, the child might not behave. This is not the permanent behavior change we want and is one of the dangers of this line of thought and intervention.

When children develop routines that are followed consistently, behaviors move from choice to habit. When this happens, adults need to prompt less with *external* enforcement because positive behaviors result from *internal* automated, ingrained patterns. This is the power of practice paired with consistency.

When children develop routines that are followed consistently, behaviors move from choice to habit.

LESSON LEARNED

Repetition leads to healthy habits.

Kids need practice in a variety of settings with a variety of individuals to strengthen their positive behaviors. And the more children practice, the more likely these behaviors will move from good choices to permanent habits.

CHAPTER TWELVE

MASTERY

I never expected to be so attuned to a dog's emotional state, but having spent so much time with LaRoux, I've become quite adept at identifying her feelings. If I interpret correctly, I know her facial expressions for happy, excited, concerned, surprised, angry, confused, tired, and content.

According to research, dogs don't experience the emotions of shame or pride, but I know one thing for sure. When LaRoux is successful at something, she seems to put forth more effort—and when she experiences fear, she tucks her tail and shuts down. Accordingly, I work hard to try to help LaRoux be successful at the tasks we undertake.

"Kennel up!" It was one of the first skills LaRoux learned and, most assuredly, the one with which she had the most success. When we left the house or when we turned in for the night, we called LaRoux to her kennel. Of course, it was set up with a comfy mat, stuffed animal, and chew toy, which encouraged her, but nonetheless, she followed our directions.

After the initial challenges I noted earlier, she was also very successful at heading outside to "do her business" rather than leaving presents on our floor, like her eldest brother, Boomer. At first, we prompted her to go outside on a regular schedule. Once there, we would point to the grass, and she seemed to know what to do. Fast-forward to now, and she just heads outside when she needs to. Happily, *practice* of this skill has made it *permanent*.

I'm certain that I'm projecting, but when LaRoux jumps in her kennel or goes out in the yard to relieve herself, she often looks back at me. If I didn't know better, I'd swear she's thinking, *Dad, look what I'm doing! Aren't you proud of me?* Okay, maybe that's a stretch, but whether it is because she is actually proud or just trying to please her dad, her success seems to drive her toward more success. And that's a great thing.

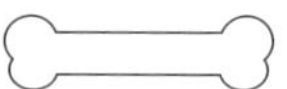

In looking again at *The Circle of Courage*, we know children need both a sense of belonging and independence in order to thrive. Additionally, as children learn and grow, they will naturally experience successes and failures. The hope is that through these experiences, children develop another trait in the model: mastery.

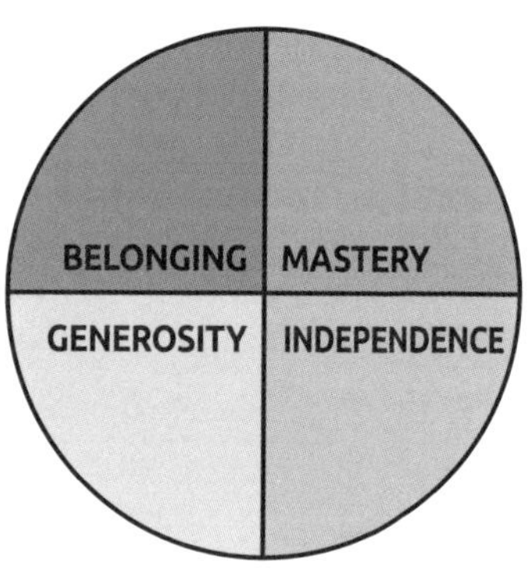

When children do something and are successful at it, they feel good about themselves and are proud of their accomplishments. The more this happens, the more open they are to try new things and the more confident they feel. This progression develops a sense of mastery in children.

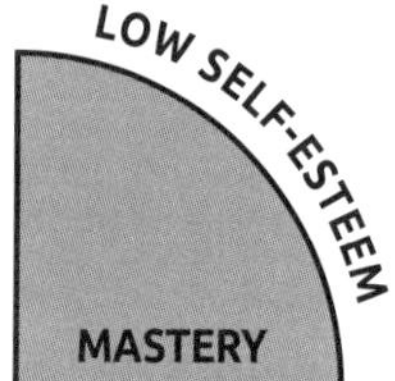

However, failure can be defeating, especially when it is experienced in excess. Children who do not find success or feel as though their efforts lead to negative outcomes can lose hope. When this happens, frustration sets in, and self-esteem can drop. We often see this in children who continually get in trouble despite their efforts to change behaviors.

Mastery is not about achieving perfection or making sure children are great at everything they do. It's about helping kids

When fostered well, a sense of mastery goes a long way in building healthy self-esteem in children.

discover and pursue their varied interests and talents through a lifelong process of learning. When fostered well, a sense of mastery goes a long way in building healthy self-esteem in children.

Mastery also contributes to kids' being more self-reliant. When children feel confident, they are more comfortable trying to solve problems. They're also more likely to face adversity with perseverance rather than giving up. Thus, they are more resilient.

Our sense of mastery develops in concert with our relationships. When we are young, we look to others to both learn and get feedback on our behaviors. The feedback we receive can contribute to us feeling confident and proud or self-conscious and uncertain. This means adult interactions are very important in helping children develop a good sense of mastery.

Because children are dependent on us to some degree, it is natural for them to seek out our input and guidance. However, if our goal is for them to be more independent in their actions, we should find ways to help them look internally rather than outwardly for validation. I learned this lesson some time ago from a very honest child.

"Mr. St. Romain, do you like my picture?" she asked me. Having heard this question from many kids over the years, I was ready with my answer. Wanting to be positive and encouraging, my knee-jerk response was always the same. "It's nice! You worked hard on that. Didn't you?"

She stopped and stared at her picture with a confused look on her face. After what seemed like an eternity of silence, she looked back at me and replied, "No. It's my scribble-scrabble. You really like it?"

As any early childhood teacher can tell you, this child obviously did not read the script we always follow in this situation. First, a child asks me if I like her drawing. Next, I tell her, "yes," which is the answer she is expecting. Then, she hands it to me, says, "I made it for you," and runs off.

This child, however, didn't seem to be seeking out my validation. She was just genuinely curious about what I thought. She had her own opinion. This interaction changed the way I handle these situations. Now when asked if I like a child's drawing, I respond, "What do **you** think about your picture? Do you like it?"

Of course, after the child shares thoughts, I try to be positive and tell them what I think. However, I want my opinion to be considered after the child's. A healthy self-concept comes from looking within, so the more I can foster internal reflection, the better chance this behavior will become a habit.

We want children to be in the habit of looking inward for self-evaluation and worth because doing so externally is very limiting.

We want children to be in the habit of looking inward for self-evaluation and worth because doing so externally is very limiting. Schools, for example, define giftedness in a very specific way. This can make very cognitively bright children feel "less than" gifted if they determine their worth based on whether they qualify for the program or not.

Howard Gardner, an American psychologist, was known for his research on *multiple intelligence*. His belief was that there is not just one fixed or singular intelligence, but rather, many ways individuals can excel. This is the mindset of mastery. We want all children to feel good about themselves and their abilities.

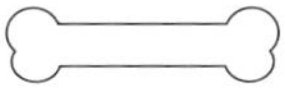

Though we want children to look internally for their self-worth and sense of mastery, it is important that, as adults, we are their advocates and cheerleaders. Rather than giving general praise, such as "Nice job," provide more specific feedback, such as "You've been working for a long time. It's so colorful and bright!" Specific feedback gives children better tools to self-evaluate their work.

For children to develop mastery, they need to be given opportunities to take on tasks independently. For young children, this could be something as simple as having them put on their shoes or push in their chairs. For older children, it could be having them make their breakfast or clean their rooms. Any task that allows them to put forth effort toward a goal can be a good mastery trait builder.

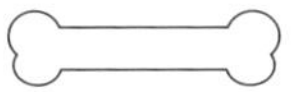

A caution, especially for parents, is the danger of "doing for." Very well-intentioned parents often provide a level of support that doesn't allow their children to experience success or failure. When we do tasks for children, we rob them of those opportunities. For example:

- Carrying young children (vs. having them walk on their own)
- Putting on children's jackets
- Picking out children's clothes to be worn

In another version of "doing for," adults intervene, keeping children from experiencing the natural consequences of their actions, which could be good learning tools to influence future behaviors:

- Cleaning up after children
- Returning home to pick up items children forgot to bring to school
- Solving problems for children

When children experience the consequences that are the result of their choices, they have the opportunity to learn. This process of learning from their successes, as well as their failures, is what leads to mastery.

Putting children in leadership roles is another way to build a sense of mastery. Although all kids can benefit from this strategy, this is especially the case for children who don't have the best self-esteem due to challenges in other areas of their lives.

Having worked at an early childhood center for many years, we routinely gave students with behavioral challenges jobs to help them feel successful and make positive contributions to our school community:

- Helping out in a classroom for students with special needs
- Running errands for teachers
- Being a buddy to a younger student

Teachers always reported this strategy as being successful. It seemed that by treating kids as positive leaders, we brought out those same qualities in them.

LESSON LEARNED

Success breeds success.

– Aristotle

We all need a sense of mastery in order to feel good about ourselves and our abilities. If we want children to develop this sense, it is critical that we provide them with diverse experiences that allow them to discover their gifts and passions. The more successful they are in their efforts, the more success will follow.

CHAPTER THIRTEEN

TIME

When LaRoux joined our family, she brought us to our self-imposed limit of six pets, with three dogs and three cats. It's always an adventure introducing a new animal to the existing group because you never quite know how they will all respond.

Our two dogs immediately accepted LaRoux, as we anticipated. [Personally, I believe they were excited about having a youngster around to stir up some trouble.] Two of our cats decided to establish permanent residence upstairs so they wouldn't have to interact with LaRoux. And given their high startle reflex and ongoing anxiety issues, this was probably for the best.

It was our third cat, Hobbs, who was the unknown variable in this equation. Truth be told, Hobbs rules the kingdom. He's very quiet and relaxed, but make no mistake, he is top of the food chain where our pets are concerned. So, we were curious to see what type of relationship he and LaRoux would have.

In their first few months of encounters, LaRoux ran around Hobbs in a tizzy, barking unceasingly. However, as time went on, behaviors settled out. LaRoux still had many social skill deficits, her biggest being respecting personal space. She barked, sniffed, licked, body-slammed, and playfully chewed on our mellow kitty's head. For the most part, though, Hobbs just ignored her.

I, on the other hand, often tried to intervene and redirect LaRoux, but my wife always stopped me. "Leave them be. They'll work it out. LaRoux's still young." Did I mention how difficult it is for me to leave *anything* be? However, I'm a good husband who knows who's at the top of the people pecking order at our house, so I did as she suggested.

Fast-forward a year, and all is well. Don't get me wrong; LaRoux occasionally oversteps her bounds and forgets her manners. But when this happens, Hobbs does not shy away from chasing her around the house and popping her with a speedy paw as a gentle reminder. It seems my wife was, yet again, right. LaRoux just needed some time.

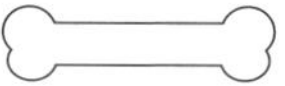

Patience has never been one of my strengths. I'm assertive. Once I know what needs to happen, I work to make it happen. I make lists and check off tasks. And I get the tasks taken care of quickly. Waiting just wastes time I could be spending making other things happen.

Time is the enemy of patience, and unfortunately for impatient adults like me, children have their own sense of time, which usually operates in two periods—*right now* and *later*. Since young children tend to live in the present, they often immerse themselves in an activity and have a hard time moving on to do future things. This is one reason transitions are challenging for some children.

Another aspect of time has to do with children's maturation and development. Although there are predictable stages of development kids pass through, the timetable for when they do so can vary from child to child. This can be very frustrating for adults.

We can't force development. The brain matures at its own pace, and trying to rush the process doesn't work. This is one of the hardest realities for teachers and parents to accept. Though I'll admit, when my children were young, I know I was guilty at times of thinking about one of them and uttering the words, "He needs to grow up."

The brain matures at its own pace, and trying to rush the process doesn't work.

This issue is made worse by our natural inclination to hold all children to a similar standard of behavior and development. This can be an especially prevalent problem in schools and daycares where children are grouped by age. I've had the same conversation repeatedly with teachers of young children about this:

"Would you come to my class to observe Kirk?" asked a teacher. "He's one of my kinder kids, and he has a very hard time during large group activities on the carpet," she continues. "He's a real mover. I think I need to have a talk with his mother."

As anticipated, I, too, noted the child had difficulty staying on the carpet when I was observing. He crawled off it (*"I'm a bear,"* he said), hopped off it (*"I'm a frog,"* he said), and at one point, slithered off it (*"I'm a snake,"* he said). When the teacher prompted him, he always came back to the carpet, but he didn't stay there and soon again needed redirecting.

When I met with the teacher, I told her I agreed with her assessment that she had "a mover" but was curious as to why she wanted to meet with his mother. She went on to explain that she was concerned he had ADHD. "Of course, I'm not a doctor," she said, "but I think mom needs to check it out. You saw my other kids. They all sit quietly at the carpet, but he's everywhere. He's going to really struggle in first grade if something doesn't change."

Though this teacher and I agreed this child seemed to have a strong need for movement, where we disagreed was in our level of concern and informal assessments. While the child's behavior stood out in her classroom, his behavior seemed very typical of many three- and four-year-old children I have observed.

Out of curiosity, I went and talked with Kirk's previous teacher and discovered that he had the same challenges in her class, with one key difference: She said she had a lot of other kids who acted just like him. I also learned that his carpet behavior of acting like an animal was part of a game they regularly played in her class during transitions.

What Kirk's kindergarten teacher wasn't acknowledging was the fact that his behavior simply could have been the result of young development. And that, given time, the behaviors would settle out. She was comparing his behavior to the behavior of the other children in her room, and because they could remain still on the carpet, she suspected his lack of being able to do so was a potential disability.

It can be frustrating when we don't see positive behavior changes in children. However, if we don't give time for behaviors to settle out, our frustrations can lead to power struggles, which then trigger continued (or worse) behaviors. Impatience can also lead to inappropriate interventions that might not be needed given the passage of time.

This is a very common story to hear, especially since the pandemic, with many children demonstrating behaviors typical at younger ages. Though it is tempting to want to "fix" the problem, we need to acknowledge that just because a child is not behaving or performing in a way we

> ***...just because a child is not behaving or performing in a way we expect—or like other children around them—doesn't mean there is a problem at all.***

expect—or like other children around them—doesn't mean there is a problem at all. It could just be an issue of time and the developing brain.

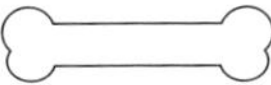

"Should I hold my child back or move him forward this year? He's an August baby. He's really smart but also very immature. I'm considering giving him the gift of another year before starting him in kindergarten. What are your thoughts?"

I have been asked this question repeatedly over the years—and my answer is always the same. In my experience, when parents are supportive and involved in their children's school experience, the child will likely be fine either way—waiting or moving forward.

However, for parents who really aren't sure what to do, I let them know that in my many years of working at an early childhood center, I've had parents who moved their children forward return to tell me their child did fine—but that they wished they would have waited one more year. However, I've never had a parent give their child the extra year and return to me, letting me know they wished they hadn't.

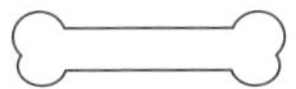

When working with children, rather than expending a great deal of energy getting them to operate on an adult timetable of stopping and starting activities quickly, it is vital to provide more time for transitions. Kids need preparation. By letting them know it's almost time to clean up, we help them learn to anticipate when activities are coming to an end. Also, when we build in more cushion time for transitions, we lower our own stress, which keeps the adults in charge more emotionally grounded.

Also, look at children's behavior through a developmental lens. Are the behaviors demonstrated typical of younger ages? If so, provide support as you would when working with younger children. In this situation, vertical planning, where teachers of different developmental levels collaborate, is a helpful strategy.

The most important of all strategies for giving children time for their developing brains to mature is that of being patient. When we try to rush the process of development, anxieties rise, and these negative emotions work against our efforts.

LESSON LEARNED

We can't force development.

Time is one variable we can't control when it comes to growth of the young brain. The best we are able to do is be patient and let development be shaped on its own timetable. It's also important to remember that the passage of time from a child's perspective is different than that of an adult's. Accordingly, we need to give kids more time in preparation for change.

CHAPTER FOURTEEN

HEALTHY RELATIONSHIPS

We'd had LaRoux for about four months when we took her on our annual trip to Galveston, Texas. We knew she would love chasing birds on the beach, experiencing the water in the Gulf of Mexico, and relaxing in the sun on the deck with her people—all of which she did. What we were not expecting was for her to have an out-of-body experience.

I took LaRoux for walks on the beach each day, and she handled being off her leash well. Though she would often run a bit ahead or behind me, she always came back when called. Whenever she encountered birds, she would chase them; whenever she encountered people, she would run toward them and then back to me. It was only the lady with the big red hat that changed this pattern.

On the fifth day of our trip, LaRoux and I headed out for our morning walk. We had established a routine of walking *down* the beach each day, so this time, I decided to take her *up*. We headed in the opposite direction to explore new territory. After walking a few subdivisions away from where we were staying, we crossed paths with another beach walker.

As the wind blew, the lady's big red hat flopped in the breeze. I am guessing something about that hat spooked LaRoux—because after running toward the lady and barking, my frantic dog looked at me in panic…and took off running as fast as her small legs would carry her. Down the beach she ran, into territory not yet explored. I called her but to no avail. She continued to run farther away, occasionally looking at me and barking louder. I felt as if she was trying to warn me, *"Don't just stand there, you fool! Run!"*

As I ran to catch up with her, I thought for sure LaRoux would eventually stop, turn around, and return to me. However, much to my surprise, she shot away from the coast and took a detour off the beach into a neighboring subdivision. By the time I caught up to the spot where I last saw her, LaRoux was gone.

As I frantically looked up and down roads for any sign of her, my phone rang. It was my wife. "Is LaRoux with you?" she asked. "She was," I said, "but something scared her, and she took off running." Before I could continue to explain, my wife interrupted. "I just found LaRoux at the back door, barking desperately to be let in," she said. "And as soon as I opened the door, she bolted straight into our bedroom and jumped up on your side of the bed. I feel certain she is looking for you."

I was in utter shock and reeling with conflicting emotions. I was relieved and happy she was safe, but also frustrated and angry she didn't follow my directions on the beach and come to me when I called. Truth be known, I was also a bit hurt that her immediate reaction when faced with a perceived threat was to abandon me and head for the hills!

"Guess I won't be taking you on any more walks this trip," I imagined myself telling LaRoux. "If you can't listen, you'll just have to stay inside while the rest of us have fun on the beach." I was ready to teach her a valuable lesson through imposed consequences. *I'll show her*, I thought.

Of course, as I walked back to the beach house, I had time to both calm down and reflect on what had just transpired. By the time I walked in and greeted LaRoux, I was no longer panicked, nor was I thinking about how I needed to respond to the incident. I was excited to see my pup. She seemed overjoyed to see me. And at that moment in time, all was right in the world.

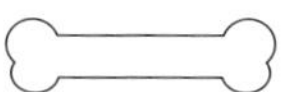

Though there was, indeed, a happy ending to the story, I continued to think about that beach incident long after its occurrence.

First of all, LaRoux amazed me. I get it. Dogs are resourceful and have good noses. But how in the world did she find her way back to the beach home? And so quickly? She was obviously in a state of distress, in completely unfamiliar territory, and hadn't been on that end of the beach before.

After spending the better part of that day obsessing about it, I came to the realization that *how* she made it back was insignificant. The important part was that she *wanted* to make it back. When LaRoux felt threatened, her instinct was to run home, where she felt safe, connected, and loved. Our relationship was her motivation.

LaRoux has gotten out of our backyard on several occasions since that beach trip—and she always returns. She doesn't come home to get a reward or avoid getting into trouble if she stays away. She does so because she cares for us. And as long as she cares, she will continue to come home. That's the long-term power of internal motivation. That's the power of the relationship.

As I continued to reflect on the beach incident, I had three behavioral revelations that all centered around one idea: motivation.

If we want to help kids make positive behavioral choices, strengthening our relationship with them is the best first step.

The first revelation? If we want to help kids make positive behavioral choices, strengthening our relationship with them is the best first step. When they trust and care for us, they have a natural internal motivation to please out of respect for the relationship.

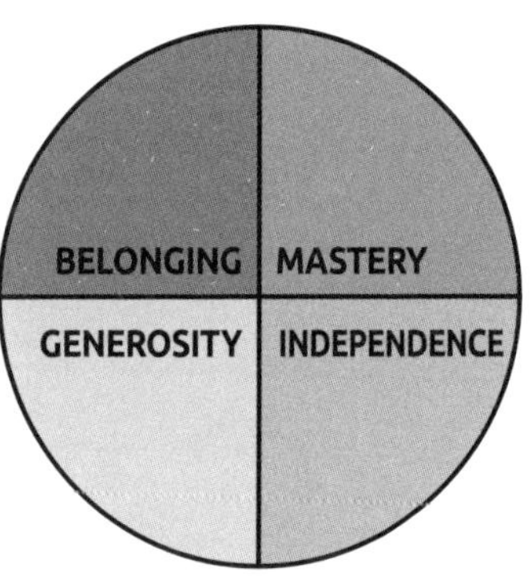

Healthy, positive relationships are an important first step in developing an ethical conscience in children. When we connect with others, we develop empathy. This empathy fosters the final trait highlighted in The Circle of Courage: Generosity. Generosity is about looking beyond our wants and needs and taking into consideration the feelings of others.

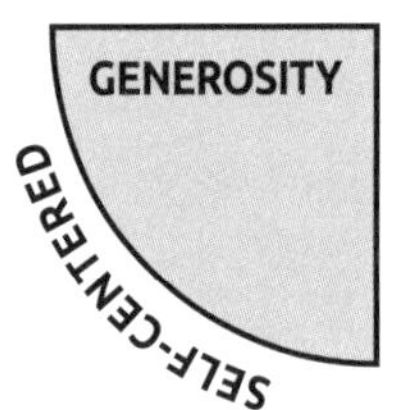

Though young children are naturally egocentric, as they get older, we want an attention shift to occur. We want their behaviors to become impacted more by connections to and relationships with others. If this doesn't happen, children can become overly focused on themselves. This can lead to a sense of entitlement, impatience, and poor social skills.

My second epiphany from that day at the beach was two-fold. I realized that young developing brains live in the present and, conversely, that adults, with our fully developed frontal lobes, tend to obsess over things and make problems seem worse than they really are.

LaRoux went from an obvious state of fight-or-flight to one of relief and joy within minutes of being let into the beach home. And that sense of joy seemed to stay with her for the remainder of the day. One minute she was running for her life, and the next, she was playing chase with herself and throwing her bone across the room with all the exuberance of what one would expect from a puppy. Based on her observable behaviors, she didn't appear to have carryover from the incident. I wish I could say the same.

With my advanced-in-age brain, I thought about the incident continuously. And the more I thought about it, the bigger an issue my brain was making of it. *What should I have done differently?* I wondered. *How can we avoid that happening again?*

The painful truth was that LaRoux had moved on, but I hadn't. Though I was happy to see her, I was also holding on to the memory of what she had done and was having difficulty letting it go.

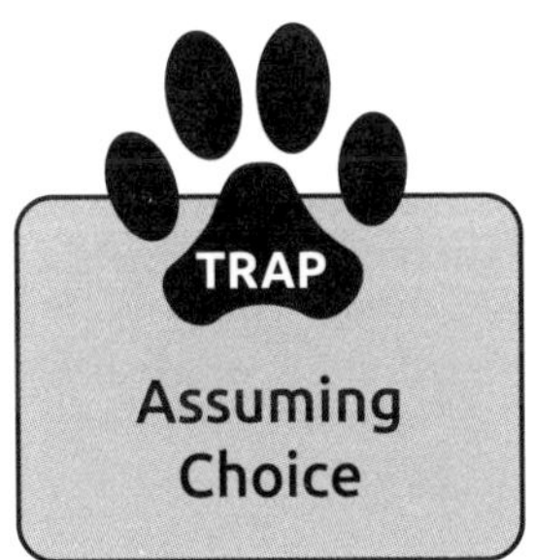

The third and final lesson I learned expands on the trap of judgment discussed in the opening chapter. When I'm confronted with misbehavior, I immediately assume choice. *I can't believe she did that*—as if she was making a conscious decision not to follow my directions and run away.

There's no doubt in my mind (now) that LaRoux didn't run away from me on the beach to be defiant or to manipulate the situation with some predetermined grand plan. She did so because she was scared. She wasn't consciously making a choice and *responding* as much as she was impulsively *reacting*. This is an important distinction.

Young frontal lobes are just beginning their long developmental journey, so they don't do much cause-and-effect advanced planning. This means young children's behaviors are most often motivated by immediate needs, meaning what's right in front of them.

> ***...young children's behaviors are most often motivated by immediate needs,...***

Sadly, when confronted with children's misbehavior, I tend to forget this. I move straight to a place of judgment, assuming they are making strategic choices based on the same level of planning skills I have—as an adult with fully developed frontal lobes. This is most often not the case.

The more I remember that misbehavior in young children most often comes from an innocent place of immediate reaction, the more patient and understanding I am in addressing concerns. This helps me stay out of power struggles and, more importantly, deal with problems in a way that doesn't damage relationships.

LESSON LEARNED

Long-term change comes from internal motivation.

The best way to create lasting positive behaviors in children is through fostering healthy relationships. When kids care for others, they develop empathy and concern. These traits serve as healthy motivators for positive behaviors that will continue long after they leave our care.

CONCLUSION

When I sat down to write this book, I thought I had identified all the lessons I learned from LaRoux through our adventures in puppy school. However, as the book unfolded, I realized I had failed to identify the most important lesson – that there will always be more lessons to learn.

Dealing with kids' behaviors can be challenging because as each day passes, the behaviors get more challenging – and our responses to them seem less effective. This is why we need to be open to change. In Einstein's words, "You can't solve today's problems with yesterday's solutions."

As I mentioned at the onset, working with children requires taking a different perspective and approach. This is what my pup, LaRoux, helped me do. She helped me become a good behavior detective by better understanding how young brains behave.

Looking at behavior through a young developmental lens helps us see how children's behaviors serve as communication. And the better we get at identifying the specific needs behind behaviors, the more equipped we will be to help kids get those needs met appropriately.

I'd love to say LaRoux was the recipient of all the lessons learned through our classes together, but as evidenced in this book, the reality is that I was the one who learned the most. Thanks, LaRoux.

ACKNOWLEDGMENTS

I'm a firm believer that animals have a "security" sense. They read people well and intuitively seem to know who they can trust: non-threatening individuals with whom they feel safe. There are several of these animal-loving people in my life who I need to acknowledge, as they either directly or indirectly contributed to this book in one way or another.

My Wife

I'm a big fan of animals, but being a high-energy type, they usually greet me with mixed reviews. I don't always have that "I'm easy to be around" nature. My wife, Prissy, on the other hand, has never met an animal who didn't gravitate toward her. Her calm and loving nature makes her an animal magnet and, thankfully, a grounding force for me.

My Children

Our boys—Matthieu, Micah, Marc, and Max—love animals, and luckily, they inherited my wife's trait for animal-whispering. Of course, my children and their interactions with our pets over the years have taught me a lot. There is no doubt in my mind we will be blessed with many grand dogs and cats in the years to come.

My Friend and Colleague

Linda Hamilton is an amazing educational consultant gifted beyond measure in understanding early childhood development. Additionally, she is a continual blessing to all the wayward animals who pass through her life, thus ending up being adopted or fostered by her. I called her on several occasions for thoughts while writing this book.

My Publishing Family

Jennifer Deshler, Robert Rabon, and the National Center for Youth Issues team have always been my cheerleaders. They are encouraging, flexible, and supportive. As I've said on many occasions, if it weren't for this group, I would most likely still be stalled in the planning stages of writing my first book.

Dog Trainers Extraordinaire

Haley Stephens and Juliette Dominguez have a gift for working well with animals and their human companions. They are patient, understanding, empathetic, and, as noted throughout the book, incredible behavior detectives with kind hearts.

Cindy Gleason Johnson and the Humane Society of Northwest Louisiana

This book would not have been written if a college friend, who volunteers at the Humane Society, had not posted about pups needing adoption. We are forever grateful for that small, kind act leading LaRoux to our family and her forever home.

Dan St. Romain

EDUCATIONAL CONSULTANT AND NATIONAL SPEAKER

Dan St. Romain is a national independent educational consultant who provides staff development and consultative services to educators and parents working with children at all developmental levels. Dan is passionate about helping individuals shift their perspective on discipline, understanding the best ways to provide support given the challenges posed in today's society.

After receiving his master's degree in education, Dan worked in both private residential and public school settings, as well as at the Region 20 Education Service Center in San Antonio, Texas. His work as a self-contained behavior unit teacher, educational diagnostician, behavior consultant, and director of a learning resource center has afforded him experience at all levels, in both general and special education settings. Dan is now enjoying semi-retirement after having worked in the school system for the past 30 years.

Dan's overwhelming strength is his skill as a presenter. Although his sessions are exceedingly interactive, his greatest asset lies in his ability to offer participants rich insight into the connectedness between educational practices and student behavior. He is the author of *Teach Skills and Break Habits: Growth Mindsets for Better Behavior in the Classroom*, *Positive Behavior Principles: Shifting Perspectives and Aligning Practices in Schools*, and several resources for teaching social skills, featuring his chameleon, Juan Pablo.

Connect with Dan at:

www.danstromain.com • dan@danstromain.com • Twitter @danstromain

About NCYI

National Center for Youth Issues provides educational resources, training, and support programs to foster the healthy social, emotional, and physical development of children and youth. Since our founding in 1981, NCYI has established a reputation as one of the country's leading providers of teaching materials and training for counseling and student-support professionals. NCYI helps meet the immediate needs of students throughout the nation by ensuring those who mentor them are well prepared to respond across the developmental spectrum.

Connect With Us Online!

@nationalcenterforyouthissues

@ncyi

@nationalcenterforyouthissues